CW00455611

RUY BLAS

THE TOWER

NOVELLAS

Alexandre Dumas

THE TOWER

Translated by Charles Wood

Victor Hugo

RUY BLAS

Translated by David Bryer

OBERON BOOKS
LONDON

First published in this collection in 2005 by Oberon Books Ltd
521 Caledonian Road, London N7 9RH
Tel: 020 7607 3637 / Fax: 020 7607 3629
e-mail: oberon.books@btinternet.com
www.oberonbooks.com

The Tower previously published in 1996

The Tower translation copyright © Charles Wood 1996, 2005

Ruy Blas translation copyright © David Bryer 2005

Introduction copyright © Nicholas Dromgoole 2005

Charles Wood is hereby identified as author of this translation
of *The Tower* in accordance with section 77 of the Copyright,
Designs and Patents Act 1988. The author has asserted his moral
rights.

All rights whatsoever in this translation of *The Tower* are strictly
reserved and application for performance etc. should be made
before commencement of rehearsal to ICM, Oxford House, 76
Oxford Street, London W1D 1BS. No performance may be
given unless a licence has been obtained, and no alterations may
be made in the title or the text of the play without the author's
prior written consent.

David Bryer is hereby identified as author of this translation of
Ruy Blas in accordance with section 77 of the Copyright, Designs
and Patents Act 1988. The author has asserted his moral rights.

All rights whatsoever in this translation of *Ruy Blas* are strictly
reserved and application for performance etc. should be made
before commencement of rehearsal to Eric Glass Ltd, 25
Ladbroke Crescent, London W11 1PS. No performance may be
given unless a licence has been obtained, and no alterations may
be made in the title or the text of the play without the author's
prior written consent.

This book is sold subject to the condition that it shall not by way
of trade or otherwise be circulated without the publisher's
consent in any form of binding or cover or circulated
electronically other than that in which it is published and
without a similar condition including this condition being
imposed on any subsequent purchaser.

A catalogue record for this book is available from the British
Library.

ISBN: 1 84002 533 6

Printed in Great Britain by Antony Rowe Ltd, Chippenham

Contents

Introduction

by Nicholas Dromgoole

The two playwrights represented here are both these days better known as authors outside the theatre. Victor Hugo (1802–85) was certainly France's greatest lyric poet throughout the nineteenth century and his poems have sturdily withstood the vagaries of time and fashion and, together with his novels, still have a wide appeal for the French reading public. Alexandre Dumas (1803–70) is nowadays best known as a popular novelist whose books still hold a place in publisher's lists, and, as with Hugo, his novels have been greedily gobbled up by Hollywood. Titles like *The Count of Monte Cristo* and *The Three Musketeers*, along with Hugo's *The Hunchback of Notre Dame* or *Les Misérables*, are still household names.

Hugo was the finer writer, but in their own time, Dumas was the better playwright. Sadly for Dumas, time has been less kind to him as a dramatist, and of the two plays published here, it is *Ruy Blas* which is more likely to hold the stage and keep its appeal for a twenty-first-century audience.

Somewhat improbably, both our authors were the sons of generals in the French revolutionary army. Hugo's father did his best to desert his wife and live with a mistress, but his wife had a determined, limpet-like quality, which meant, that in spite of the general's best efforts, she and her children followed him when he was posted to the conquering French army in Spain, Hugo therefore not only spoke tolerable Spanish, but also had a reasonable grounding in Spanish history and culture.* This does not mean that the play *Ruy Blas* has more than a very

---

* This is all the more remarkable since, although he spent eighteen years in exile in the English Channel Islands, he never learned English, and remained wonderfully naïve about most of his host country's manners and traditions, judging by works like *L'Homme qui rit* which is supposedly set in England. He was a neighbour of my own great, great grandfather, a Captain Nicholas Dromgoole, by then an elderly veteran who had fought in Wellington's army at Waterloo, but that battle was at best a tricky subject, since Hugo idolised Napoleon, in spite of the fact that he was in exile as a result of his detestation of the Emperor Napoleon III.

tenuous relationship with actual Spanish history. Like Dumas, Hugo regarded the past very much as something to be re-written, re-invented and altogether manipulated in the interest of creating a worthwhile stage drama. Hugo, famous for the number and variety of his amatory adventures, was as cheerfully unfaithful to history as he was to his own wife.

France's own nineteenth-century history was much more chequered than most people realise. Hugo lived through an astonishing period of political instability. The eighteenth century had been a ferment of political controversy, finally culminating in the French Revolution of 1789, which had gone woefully out of control. The King was executed, as were all too many of his former subjects, in the orgy of executions by the guillotine known as the Terror. Not only did Napoleon then establish himself as emperor (not quite what the revolutionaries had originally had in mind!), but he then set about conquering the rest of Europe. Whatever else may be said about Napoleon, he certainly sacrificed depressingly large numbers of French lives on his various battlefields, to say nothing of cheerfully deserting one army in Egypt and another on the retreat from Moscow. Hugo was thirteen when Napoleon was finally defeated at Waterloo. During the rest of his life France was somehow trying to pick up the pieces and establish a stable form of government. The Bourbon monarchy was restored in 1815, but fell from power in 1830. After that revolution Louis Philippe reigned as king until 1848, when another revolution ousted him and established a temporary republic, overthrown by a coup d'état in which Napoleon III established himself as emperor. His reign lasted until 1870 and France's defeat in the Franco-Prussian war. A republic was then set up which finally provided a generally acceptable, democratically elected form of government. Hugo died in 1885, a national idol and by then a national institution. These political changes were very far from being marginal. This was not just a case of one government being replaced by another. Each change was an immense upheaval, hordes of people losing their livelihoods, deaths on the streets, a whole superstructure of power shattered and replaced, with new people in charge, making lists of the proscribed, settling old scores, condemning former dignitaries to death, prison or exile. And all these changes took place in Hugo's lifetime. It is not surprising that political beliefs were potentially dangerous to hold, and could sometimes quite literally put lives at risk.

Society was changing too. The agricultural and industrial revolutions were even more far-reaching than any political changes. The population of France was expanding at an astonishing rate; new industrial cities were altering a whole way of life as more and more people manned the growing factory system. The old social hierarchy of aristocrats and peasants was increasingly eroded by the steady growth of a newly-prosperous middle class. The women in this class came to represent the first mass consumer demand for entertainment from the media. Lending libraries, newspapers, magazines, a growing flood of novels, opera, ballet and above all drama in large new theatres expanded to meet this new demand. The education and standards of the women who had leisure and money in the new middle class were not impressive. The arts had to change to meet the new demand, and cultural historians call these changes in the arts 'Romanticism'. The concept of romantic love, radical political extremism, sentimentality, escapism, sensationalism, a demand for exciting extremes, and a new sense of being alienated from the surrounding industrial culture: these made up the new 'Romantic' ideology.

Hugo, while embodying all these changes, was doing something more. He wanted to change the conventions of literature and particularly of drama. In view of the political upheavals France experienced in the early nineteenth century it is not surprising that 'romanticism' arrived a little late on the cultural scene. What Wordsworth and the English Romantic poets had done with the writing of poetry at the end of the eighteenth century, Hugo set about doing for French verse in the 1830s and 40s. Much the same applied to drama. Schiller had been made an honorary member of the French revolutionary assembly for his play *The Robbers*, written as early as 1781. With the *Sturm und Drang* movement, German Romanticism had flourished from then onwards. Yet in 1827, with the preface to his play *Cromwell*, Hugo was breaking new ground in French theatre. The preface is now seen as a manifesto for what the new Romantic drama was to attempt. The play was not intended to be performed (it would have lasted at least six hours!), but to be read and thus to avoid the heavy censorship exercised over French drama. Its preface acted as a clarion call for an attack on the kind of play still holding the stage at that bastion of the traditionalists, France's national theatre, the Comédie Française.

Paying due homage to Shakespeare, Hugo wanted to do away with the dramatic unities, and to loosen the rigid categories of genres, so that a play could be part tragedy and part comedy with aspects both of the 'sublime' and the 'grotesque' and so closer to real life. He advocated verse drama, but wanted to free the rhythms of the alexandrine and avoid an artificial poetic diction, using words from everyday speech that were not considered 'poetic' by the traditionalists. He felt that historical drama, rather than simply playing on the clashes of major personalities, should attempt to give a sense of its period. What he did not say, but certainly set about doing, was to use history as a means of avoiding censorship and as a covert way of commenting to the audience on current political events and controversies.

His play *Hernani* at the Théâtre-Français in 1830 tried to do all these things, and has gone down as a milestone in French theatre history for causing a riot on its first night. It should however be remembered that Hugo was not outrageously new. The theatres of the Paris boulevards had been performing melodramas for years to popular acclaim. They cheerfully ignored the unities, mixed genres and positively wallowed in distortions of history to give exciting and sensational incident after incident. What Hugo was doing was to take this popular and rather despised form of drama into the hallowed precincts of French classical drama, still haunted by the shades of Racine, Moliere, Voltaire, Marivaux and Beaumarchais, Together with Dumas, he made the form of historical melodrama respectable, popular, and gave it an appeal to the serious theatre-goer, not only by the quality of its writing, but also by an attempted insight into the motivations and personalities of its chief characters.

In his preface to *Ruy Blas*, he divides his audience into three parts; the thinkers who want insight into why the characters act as they do, the women who want passions and feelings, preferably amatory, and the majority who just want exciting action. He has the grace to admit later on that women can also be thinkers too. His play tries to meet all these requirements. It was not a great success when first presented in 1838, but when Sarah Bernhardt revived it in 1871 it ran for 300 performances and was considered one of her major roles.

Originally it only made it to the stage at all when the Duc d'Orleans, then heir to the French throne, asked the Prime Minister, Guizot, to grant both Hugo and Dumas the right to have their plays performed in a new playhouse, the Théâtre de la Renaissance, a right given to no other playwrights at the time. The play takes place in seventeenth-century Madrid. A Spanish nobleman blames the Queen for his banishment, after he has seduced one of the Queen's ladies-in-waiting. Learning that his valet, Ruy Blas, nurses a hopeless passion for the Queen, he plans a Machiavellian revenge. He passes off his valet at court as a distant relative, and at court Ruy Blas powerfully champions the cause of the poor and dispossessed, as well as winning a place in the Queen's affections. The tantalizing possibility of social justice, the Queen's support, and a possible seduction are then blown sky high by the nobleman's return to reveal all. The aristocrat is killed in finely messy style by Ruy Blas who then takes poison in a splendidly romantic gesture before the Queen herself. He kills himself because he is only a valet, and so has no hope of achieving what was almost within his grasp.

While the iron hierarchies of nineteenth-century social strata no longer seem quite so daunting to a modern audience, the valet must have been rather less than totally convincing even in 1838. He is clearly not so much a valet as Victor Hugo himself in populist dress, standing up for the people's rights, championing the cause of romantic liberty, and not at all unwilling to cast a predatory and erotic eye at a pretty woman quite regardless of her royal rank. As one of the leaders of the Romantic Movement, it is as a champion of the people's rights that Hugo managed to project himself throughout his long career. As he himself says in his preface to *Ruy Blas*:

> Below the nobility...there can be seen stirring in the shadows something huge, dark, and unknown. It is the people. The people, to whom the future belongs, not the present; the people, orphaned, poor, intelligent and strong; brought very low, and aspiring very high; bearing on their backs the signs of servitude, and in their hearts the beginnings of genius; the people, serfs of the great lords, and, in their misery and their abasement, in love with what to them, in the midst of this decayed society, represents authority, charity and fruitfulness with a divine radiance. The people should be represented in the character of Ruy Blas.*

Hugo's public had no radio, no films, no television, so that if they wanted to see fiction acted out by real people, the theatre was all there was. This meant that what is now distributed among so many different media, had somehow to be covered by theatre alone, catering in effect for a much more diverse audience than modern theatre. It meant, too, that the gossip, rumour and scandal that are the staple of the modern tabloid press, could not cover radio, film and television personalities, since these did not exist, and nor did the sports stars on whom the tabloids batten so voraciously today. Yet the gutter press increasingly flourished throughout the nineteenth century, and while royalty, the aristocracy, the rich and famous were its targets then and as now, theatre people, and writers like Dumas and particularly Hugo, were all too often the sacrificial lambs

* Anybody reading the published diaries of the American playwright, Clifford Odets, so fashionable in the 1930s, will notice that like much of the literary, artistic and academic intelligentsia of his time, he looked forward to an inevitable communist revolution which would replace capitalist injustice with what was clearly for him a utopian communism. For modern readers his generation seems sadly uninformed and naïve. It is the same with the Romantics of the 1830s and 1840s. For them 'the people' was an abstraction, which all the same sparked off radical new thinking about society. In *Ruy Blas* the summons to 'the people' was undoubtedly for Hugo, a clarion call to action. It did not matter that nobody was quite clear what the action should be!

led to press slaughter. The tabloids of his time immediately suggested a sub-text for *Ruy Blas*. In 1837 Hugo had been asked to attend a Versailles reception to celebrate the marriage of the heir to the throne, the Duc d'Orléans. The Duchess, Helena von Mecklenburg-Schwerin, proved to be a great admirer of Hugo's poetry and could recite some of it by heart. Hugo found new and powerful friends. He rose in the Légion d'Honneur, and was presented with a large oil painting by the married couple. The Duke persuaded Guizot to allow Hugo and Dumas to present their plays at a new, up-to-date theatre. This was all too much for the tabloids. Clearly the valet Ruy Blas stood for Hugo himself, and the Queen in the play, it was suggested, was acting out the role of the real life Duchess. Here was a whiff of scandal indeed. Nothing has ever been proved, but some writers certainly imply that the smoke surrounding this episode may indeed have emanated from some real fire.

This is only one of the many enigmas that surround Hugo. He had an amazing gift for catching media attention and generally living at the centre of a blaze of publicity. What separated Hugo from so many who temporarily hug the headlines, were his major talents as a poet, playwright and novelist. He consistently delivered. He stayed in the headlines because of the sheer quality of what he produced. Yet as he attitudinized, struck poses, postured in this or that guise, he antagonized many who, while grudgingly forced to accept his quality as a creative artist, still saw him as a kind of mountebank playing up for the media. His English biographer Graham Robb perceptively refers to 'a limited liability company of egos, each one feeding off the other and maintained by an army of commentators'. Jean Cocteau wittily summed him up, maintaining: 'Victor Hugo was a madman who believed he was Victor Hugo'.

Already by the time *Ruy Blas* appeared, Hugo's fame and position were secure. His audience came to see the work of a man they already admired, someone very much in the public eye. They were not disappointed. It is Hugo the poet who consistently underpins the dramatic success of this play. Not until the end of the century, with Edmund Rostand's *Cyrano de*

Bergerac (1898), would any other French playwright come near Hugo's grandly inventive approach to the alexandrine. Not only is the language a constant joy, it is so finely attuned that it should be possible, once the listener knows the characters involved, to tell who is speaking just from the subtle differences in the way each character expresses this glorious poetry. David Bryer's translation for this volume, though written in iambic pentameters – not alexandrines – and rhyming only at certain, selected moments, impressively preserves much of Hugo's nuanced, character-driven style.

Yet all the time Hugo is evidently aware of the majority of the audience he defines so clearly in his preface, the majority who thirst for exciting action, who want things to happen and to happen quickly. There is a parallel with much the same dilemma when the English romantic poet, Samuel Taylor Coleridge, wrote his very successful play *Remorse* in 1816. Like Hugo, Coleridge was heavily influenced by Shakespeare's achievements, particularly by the subtle and revealing way Shakespeare shows the development of character, not only by the soliloquies which allow an audience to enter into a character's innermost thoughts, but by the dramatic action which moulds character and displays a personality changing and growing as a response to the pressure of events. Yet the fashion of the day for Coleridge too was for caricatures rather than characters, for sensational events rather than subtleties, for simple set pieces rather than complexities. Somehow if he was to be successful and yet not altogether lose sight of his aim to analyse real people, Coleridge had to strike a balance between these two almost opposing forces, between melodrama and spectacle on the one hand and poetry, complexity of personality and believable situations on the other. *Remorse* and *Ruy Blas* represent an uneasy compromise between the two forces. Coleridge wanted to study the effect of remorse on an individual and thus appeal to the 'thinkers' in his audience. Hugo is more concerned with serious reflections on the nature of political power. Sadly nobody has had the courage to revive *Remorse* this or last century, while *Ruy Blas* continues to hold the stage with mesmerizing force whenever – and wherever –

it is revived. Amazingly, it has never been performed in Britain, unless one counts the three-act version created as a vehicle for Mrs Patrick Campbell in the 1920s. (It is to be hoped that Bryer's fresh, vigorous translation can change this depressing statistic!) Nowadays it is saved from oblivion by its poetry, by its ideas, and by the truth of its characters' emotions. In 1838 these probably held it back a little and it was only the humour of its comic scenes and the pace and excitement of its melodrama that really appealed. How useful for posterity that Hugo was a sufficiently great poet to appeal at so many levels, and still have so much to offer a modern audience.

With Dumas, this is less true. Like Hugo, he had everything going for him. His parentage seems almost too aptly prepared for the Romantic Movement. Not only was his father a general in the revolutionary army, and his grandfather an aristocrat, his grandmother had been a black slave in San Domingo. Even Lord Byron's background seems positively pallid in comparison. In the annals of French literature, the Alexandre Dumas who wrote *The Three Musketeers* and *The Tower* is known as Dumas *père*, because his illegitimate son, Dumas *fils*, became in his turn the celebrated author of *La Dame aux Camélias*.

By the time he wrote the *The Three Musketeers* in 1845, still undoubtedly his best-known novel, and still very much in print, Dumas *père* had become not so much an individual writer as almost an industry, and it is still debatable just how much that book owes to the efforts of others. It is based, event by event and far too closely for artistic respectability, on *The Memoirs of Monsieur d'Artagnan, Captain-Lieutenant of the First Company of the King's Musketeers* by Gatien de Courtilz, published in 1700. A record is kept in the Marseilles library that Dumas took the book out in 1843 and never returned it. Even so he collaborated loosely with Auguste Maquet on the book. To be fair, when Dumas had previously wanted to acknowledge another such collaboration, his publisher refused. 'Anything signed Alexandre Dumas is worth three francs a line – sign it Dumas and Maquet and it won't fetch thirty sous a line' .

Naturally as Dumas became ever more famous, his collaborators resented their anonymity. In 1845 a pamphlet attacking him was published entitled, 'Manufacture of Romantic Novels – The Firm of Alexandre Dumas and Co', purporting to tell all.

So it is not surprising to learn that *The Tower*, written in 1832, and Dumas' most famous play, also had similarly murky origins. It was based on a play by an aspiring writer Frederick Gaillardet, who had given his manuscript to Harel, the manager of the Théâtre de la Porte-Saint Martin, where Dumas had already had great success with his historical melodrama *Anthony* in 1831. Harel first asked the critic Janine to attempt a rewrite, but then asked Dumas to see what could do with the play. Still on a sick bed after a cholera epidemic, Dumas duly 'improved' the play, and even generously offered to take only a fee, leaving the authorship to Gaillardet alone. Harel preferred to advertise the play as by a set of asterisks, and Frederick Gaillardet, and then after suitable haggling agreed with Gaillardet to put the young man's name first, and then the asterisks. He then busily spread the real name of the second author by word of mouth. The play was a great success and Dumas henceforward insisted on including it in any list of his own works. Ultimately he and Gaillardet fought a duel, pistols not swords, over Gaillardet's claim that the play was really his. Neither managed to hit the other. The play continued a hit for 800 performances and was constantly revived. Years later, Gaillardet asked that the name of Dumas should be coupled with his at a revival in recognition of 'the large part this incomparable talent had in the success of the play'. Posterity has been unkind to Gaillardet. There is no doubt we now think of the play as belonging very much to Dumas; and like the whole tribe of the other collaborators of Dumas, Gaillardet has largely sunk from sight.

Scurrilous pamphlets, duels, rival claims from disgruntled collaborators, none of these affected Dumas' growing reputation, nor his ever-increasing public. Dumas learned his trade as a writer in the competitive and demanding world of the commercial theatre. He began by writing for vaudeville, but just as Hector Berlioz was overwhelmed by the visit of and English theatre company playing Shakespeare to Paris in 1829, inspiring his *Symphonie Fantastique*, so they opened up fresh vistas for Dumas as well. He had of course already read Hugo's preface to *Cromwell* in 1827. Berlioz fell even more heavily for a young actress in the company, Harriet Smithson, than he did for Shakespeare, marrying her in 1833 and emerging disillusioned from their relationship nine years later, but with his allegiance to Shakespeare undimmed. Dumas had the artistic acumen and imagination to realize that the new Romanticism inaugurated by Hugo and historical drama were made for each other, and his *Henri III et sa cour* (1829) was perhaps the first triumph of Romantic theatre. This, alongside other plays by Dumas busily scurrying back down the corridors of time for sensation and scandal, put him at the forefront of the Romantic movement and brought him the friendship not only of Victor Hugo but also of Alfred de Vigny.

Recognising the creation of a new French theatrical genre – historical melodrama – Dumas, on a rising tide of affluence, built and financed a Théâtre Historique, but like so many creative artists, his ambitions outreached his grasp of finance and, continually in debt in spite of his huge earnings, he saw his creation fail in 1850. Yet throughout his literary career he never deserted the theatre. Better known in the twentieth century for his novels, in fact he wrote almost a hundred plays, even turning many of his novels into subsequent plays. Even as a novelist he never lost sight of the theatre's immediacy. His effects are largely theatrical effects: one almost hears at the end of a chapter the audience's sudden gasp of surprise at the final twist, the last effective line before the curtain trundles down. It was not where he got his material, nor who assembled it for him, so much as what Dumas did with it that mattered. The name of Dumas was worth three francs a line because his touch was unique. 'Nobody had read every Dumas book or seen every Dumas play, that would be almost as impossible as for any one person to have written every Dumas book and play – but everybody had read some Dumas.' – 'If a Robinson Crusoe exists in 1850 he must surely be about to read the *Three Musketeers*.' – The world, including France, learned its French history from Dumas.' 'Does Dumas make you think? Hardly ever. Dream? Never. But turn page after compulsive page? Always!'

He was a great populariser of Romanticism. This new movement in art turned its back on the Industrial Revolution, then transforming the cities in which the artists of Romanticism actually lived, as they sought excitement in tear-jerking emotions, sentimental love at first sight, the macabre, the frightening and supernatural, indeed almost anything that got away from the present – other cultures, other times, from medieval Scotland and oriental fantasy to historical romance.

The very industrialism that art largely ignored created a new middle-class audience rich but far less discriminating and less demanding than the smaller more exclusively educated class an author could have expected in the previous century. Dumas was writing for a mass readership, the first in history, and he gave them colourful, exciting heroics dressed up in the trappings of the past. *The Tower* is a prime example of what became for him a well-tried formula.

One of the first questions today's audience will want answered is just how true Dumas' account is to the actual historical facts as we know them. It is one thing for Shakespeare, in the name of dramatic licence, to massage and manipulate events and people to an order acceptable within the confines of the stage, the three to four hours of the performance, and the limits of the dramatically possible. With the understandable exception of *Richard III*, Shakespeare gave his audience a set of guidelines to enable them to understand and appreciate what had actually happened in the past. In his historical plays he was recreating a sense of national identity from a retelling of events that were much closer to real life than to myth. Dumas was doing nothing so acceptable. He was rewriting, creating a set of bogus events, that bore almost no relation at all to the actual facts that history recorded, and his aim was to sensationalise, to startle his audience with horrific scandals and events.

It is true that the prestige of the French throne at the beginning of the fourteenth century was affected by the scandals associated with Philip the Fair's three daughters-in-law, Marguerite of Burgundy (married to the future Louis X), Jeanne of Poitiers (married to the future Philip V) and Blanche of the

Marche (married to the future Charles IV). Jeanne's innocence was established and proclaimed by a parlement, but Blanche and Marguerite were convicted of having had as lovers two gentlemen-in-waiting, Philippe and Gaultier d'Aulnay, who were duly executed. The two princesses were imprisoned in solitary confinement in the Château Gaillard. In due course, Blanche entered a nunnery. Marguerite became an embarrassment when her husband later mounted the throne and wished to marry Clementia, daughter of the King of Hungary. Rather than face long, drawn-out negotiations with the papacy for a royal divorce, Louis X had his wife smothered in her cell between two mattresses. How enthusiastic his second wife was to ally herself with such a Bluebeard history has not recorded, although Louis X was known to his people as Louis the Quarrelsome. Not the sort of husband a wife was likely to pick a quarrel with.

This incident, a royal princess committing adultery with a courtier, has been inflated by Dumas in *The Tower* into an astounding series of events. Marguerite, presented as Queen, has had two children by a former lover. He re-appears and blackmails her into giving him high office, but both are unaware that the two children, far from being put to death, are in fact none other than the two gentlemen in waiting, Philippe and Gaultier d'Aulnay, who both die in suitably lurid circumstances with a great deal of the nineteenth-century equivalent of tomato ketchup liberally bedaubing everything and everyone in sight.

As with farce, to which it is closely allied, melodrama is a theatrical genre whilch developed its own conventions. Characters are simplified and exaggerated, the good are absurdly good, and in just as much caricature the bad are unbelievably bad. To be effective the genre requires a swift-moving plot, full of unexpected twist and turns. It may be almost impossible-to-believe moments such as:

> (*Enter GAULTIER covered in blood.*)
> GAULTIER: Marguerite…I give you back the key to the tower…
> MARGUERITE: Gaultier, I am your mother.

GAULTIER: My mother? My mother?
(*Horror – His hand and arm out to curse her.*)
Then be damned!
(*Gaultier dies.*)

But the swift moving narrative dealing out fresh surprises in spades, obviously carried its nineteenth-century audience inexorably onwards and away into a never-never land of thrills and fantasies.

Even in the brief extract above, one virtue of the play as presented here is very clear. Charles Wood's lean, rhythmic language makes the most of the drama and of Dumas (if indeed it is Dumas and not Gaillardet), and loses none of the fun.

For a modern audience scenes like these are hard to take. Already by the 1890s Oscar Wilde could say of Dickens that 'One must have a heart of stone to read the death of Little Nell without laughing'. Whereas Dickens still succeeds as a writer at a variety of levels – even if his sentimentality can seem mawkish – Dumas seems less rich. At the level of exciting boy's adventure stories, his books and plays still work – Dumas actually took one of his plots from Fenimore Cooper – but these days an adult readership expects a more perceptive approach to characters than Dumas' broad outlines of people. Rather than developing, changing, being affected by events and maturing as they interact with one another, Dumas' characters tend to remain the same from beginning to end. They are goodies and baddies at the start and they come to their inevitable good or bad ends at the finish with a certain predictability. It is, to use Coleridge's term, difficult to suspend our disbelief.

It is only with an indulgent smile at the excesses of mid-nineteenth century melodrama, once beloved by its less demanding audience, but now impossibly dated, that we can span the gap between ourselves and the different expectations of over a hundred and seventy years ago. This only applies to melodrama. We are not as yet cut off to the same extent from a whole range of other Victorian arts, but we have lost their taste, in that first flush of Romanticism, for melodrama. Dumas began in the theatre where melodrama then reigned supreme, and the sure knowledge of what would 'go with the public', of exactly what they wanted, was once his main strength. Paradoxically to some, it is now his weakness. Melodrama is out of fashion. Yet perhaps if we can learn to view these cardboard heroes of outdated fiction with that indulgent smile, we will realize the very solid virtues Dumas still possesses. The fun and excitement of a fast moving story, a boyish enthusiasm for heroes and bravery which never quite leaves any of us, the deft turn and turn-about of a plot that is still easy to follow, the colour and romance of a nostalgic past.

Even today whenever the weather gets rough at sea, the Greek fishermen of Lemnos, hoping to calm the evil spirit of Alexander the Great's mother, thought to be blindly seeking her son in the heart of the storm, shout into the wind: 'Alexander still lives!' Through all the vicissitudes of changing fashion, as the years have hurtled by, Alexandre Dumas still lives too, books in print, plays still performed. Audience's perceptions and expectations may have changed but in the works of Dumas and Victor Hugo too, at the heart of the Romantic storm, something is still very much alive.

THE TOWER

(La Tour De Nesle)

For my brother Peter
once a true swashbuckler

Characters

MARGUERITE DE BOURGOGNE

BURIDAN

GAULTIER D'AULNAY

PHILIPPE D'AULNAY

ORSINI

LANDRY

SAVOISY

DE PIERREFONDS

DE MARIGNY

LOUIS X

RAOUL

CHARLOTTE

VEILED WOMAN

NECROMANCER

POURSUIVANT at ARMS

SERGEANT

ARBALÉTRIER

BOATMAN

JEHAN

RICHARD

SIMON

Guards, Courtiers, Lords, Petitioners

The action of the play takes place in Paris in 1314

This version of *The Tower* was first performed by the Almeida Theatre Company, at the Almeida Theatre, London on 8 December 1995, with the following cast:

MARGUERITE DE BOURGOGNE, Sinead Cusack

BURIDAN, Adrian Dunbar

GAULTIER D'AULNAY, Ben Miles

PHILIPPE D'AULNAY, John Light

ORSINI, David Herlihy

LANDRY, Nigel Lindsay

SAVOISY, Geoffrey Beevers

DE PIERREFONDS, Tim McMullan

DE MARIGNY / LOUIS X, Iain Mitchell

RAOUL, Hugh Simon

CHARLOTTE, Cate Hamer

SIMON, Perry Benson

RICHARD, Gregory Donalchon

AN ARBALÉTRIER, Derren Litten

JEHAN / OLIVIER / POURSUIVANT AT ARMS,
Michael Hodgson

Director, Howard Davies
Designer, John Napier
Lighting, Mark Henderson
Music, Jonathan Dove
Fights, Williarn Hobbs
Sound, John A Leonard

ACT ONE

Scene 1

The banks of the River Seine.

Double tower of the Tour de Nesle, a hidden quay and steps up from the river. City wall. Gate of Saint Honoré. Boats.

Heard off: fanfare. Drums, trumpets, bagpipes and cymbals. Clamour of horse, foot, shout. Civic entry of MARGUERITE DE BOURGOGNE, soon to be Queen of France. Horses, lances, banners shadows across the scene. A crescendo of noise and then fading.

Enter PHILIPPE D'AULNAY, a young squire from the Flanders war – gambeson, white cross of France, belt, sword, dagger and purse, hose, short boots, spurs – excited by what he's seen.

Enter a VEILED WOMAN.

> VEILED WOMAN
> *Mon jeune seigneur!*

> PHILIPPE
> *Oui?*

> VEILED WOMAN
> I must speak secretly.

> PHILIPPE
> I cannot hear, drums, music still
> in my ears. Our Queen has entered
> Paris and I have just seen her, my
> brother, Gaultier at her side.
>
> Him, I could not see for bright
> steel, gold, silver…sumpture.
>
> But side her he rode, captain of
> her guard… I… I…am come to
> Paris…for good or ill.

(*The clamour fades.*)

> Proud queen... I know she saw me.
> (*He strikes a pose.*)
> 'I've caught her eyes. All must
> exclaim: the loveliest heard or
> seen is she!'

(*The procession has gone.*)

> There, what do you say to that?
> (*Laughing, he beckons.*)
> I can hear you now, whatever you
> would say...say it.
> (*He listens to her.*)
> Oh! *Oui, oui...* I am?
>
> I am sure that I am and if she is
> beautiful...?
> (*He listens affronted.*)
> Woman! I never break a *rendezvous,*
> desert a friend, refuse a breach or
> disappoint a lady does me honour...

VEILED WOMAN

Your hand! A man will ask to see
your hand...
(*She gives him something.*)
...on which...this ring.

PHILIPPE

Merci, ma gracieuse.

VEILED WOMAN

Adieu mon soldat!
(*Going.*) *Plaisir et courage!*

(*Exit VEILED WOMAN. PHILIPPE laughs.*)

PHILIPPE

Eh bien.
First I shall write to my brother.

(*Exit PHILIPPE.*)

(*A shout from the city wall, an ARBALÉTRIER, crossbowman, in his pepperpot or sentry box.*)

ARBALÉTRIER

There floats another!

(*Enter SERGEANT, in a boat with two BOATMEN.*)

SERGEANT

There!
(*To BOATMEN.*)
See it...your hooks.

(*Leaping ashore, and the ARBALÉTRIER down from his pepperpot, they drag out the body of a young man by way of the steps and the quay.*)

ARBALÉTRIER

Find more. It is always three.

(*He crosses himself.*)

SERGEANT

You are safe for your vile visage.
(*Back in the boat.*)
*Oui...la lune...*see it? Another
pretty young man...see it, get
out to it...*un fleurant...un
vasistas*...oh shameful, wasteful.

BOATMAN

It will not escape us...
(*Rowing.*) ...it is rare they swim with
throats cut – not even fish.

(*ARBALÉTRIER drags away the slime wet dead body of the young man who is without his hose, throat cut.*)

(*Exit SERGEANT and BOATMEN in boat.*)

Scene 2

ORSINI's tavern at the gate of Saint Honoré.

PHILIPPE writing at a table. The tavern full. The pot boy LANDRY, JEHAN. Shoemaker, RICHARD with SIMON a fisherman, both have had a lot of wine. ORSINI serving OTHERS, stopped by them.

SIMON
The count?

ORSINI
What?

SIMON
Drowned rats this morning?

RICHARD
I said he was to ask Orsini because
if 'tis to do with the devil he
will know...

ORSINI
Three.

RICHARD
I said he would know, it would
surprise me not if...

SIMON
All noble, young and pretty?

RICHARD
...he pushed them in. He is evil
is Orsini – say so, say... Evil?

ORSINI
Three fine young men, good names,
comely, less than a week in Paris.

RICHARD
It is always the same. I swear he
poisons them. Orsini?

ORSINI
I do not.

SIMON

One thing...the devil, whoever
the devil is, and he is a devil to
spill young blood, this – he knows
who to pick.

RICHARD

Oui.
(*Savouring.*)
The highest in the land, their very
fruit of their very loins – tender
necks ripped open and slid into the
Seine...

ORSINI

That is truth.

RICHARD

...and...all in the same stretch
of river, below the Tower of Nesle.

ORSINI

That is truth. Will you drink
more?

RICHARD

I will do...but who? Who does it
to these poor young valiant pretty
young fish?

ORSINI

I know not.

SIMON

You know not?
Orsini you know everything filthy
and evil, poisonous, malodorous,
diabolical, shunned by polite
Christians...you are familiar in
every way for, you...know witches,
consort with them – suck their paps...
paps...
(*Loves the thought.*) ...paps.

31

PHILIPPE

Maître!

ORSINI

I know nothing.

SIMON

Nothing? I know you ought answer
that young man does you the honour.
I myself would not be so...

PHILIPPE

Maître!

SIMON

(*Indicating the letter he writes.*)
... Civil, but then...

ORSINI

Messire?

SIMON

... I know you.

PHILIPPE

One of your pot boys... I shall give
him a sou will he take this for
me...two?

(*PHILIPPE signs the letter with a flourish, a grin at ORSINI.*)

ORSINI

Landry!

(*LANDRY, a huge brute of a man, quondam sergeant, quilted jacket with faded white cross, an arbalétrier's belt with spanning hook, a double dagger sheath, footless and dangling separate hose, bare feet – has lurked listening.*)

LANDRY

Sous parisis?

PHILIPPE

Oui...

ORSINI

Take it.

RICHARD

I cannot believe him... I cannot
believe you Orsini.

ORSINI

I care not – what you believe.

(*PHILIPPE addresses the letter. LANDRY is waiting.*)

SIMON

Was I foul named Orsini, tavern
keeper of a filthy tavern so close
to the old Tower of Nesle which it
is, I would know...

RICHARD

If I had windows looked out, as
yours do Orsini, I would only need
look out at night and see every
thing in the river, slid in...

SIMON

I would have no surprise you have
plucked a few purses out, looped to
belts strapped about fine rich
pretty young drowned fish *first*,
Orsini, before any with boat and
grapple, for you are a very evil
very sly Italy villain.

ORSINI

I am not a villain. Nor of the
night watch...

RICHARD

The devil you are a villain!

ORSINI

I am an innkeeper.

SIMON

Then, as well, go to him – the
devil!

ORSINI

On instant you let go me I shall.
Do you want more wine?

SIMON

Yes I do want more wine. At once!

(*SIMON tosses down a coin. ORSINI picks it up.*)

ORSINI

Inside whose purse have you been
fishing?

(*ORSINI exits.*)

SIMON

What! I am an honest man!

RICHARD

You are, Simon.

SIMON

Twice today I have been called
thief!

PHILIPPE

To my brother, at the Louvre, his
name… Gaultier d'Aulnay.

SIMON

You say his name?

(*LANDRY goes with the letter.*)

PHILIPPE

You know him?

(*SIMON stands, sways slightly as if about to say something,
then sits down again, sniggers to RICHARD.*)

SIMON

He asks do we know him?

RICHARD

Saw you the procession into Paris?

SIMON

You ask me, Richard?

PHILIPPE

The Queen... I saw.

RICHARD

With sisters, the Princesses Jeanne
and Blanche?

(*JEHAN joins them.*)

SIMON

I saw it. He says, 'I saw it...'

JEHAN

(*Spits.*) I saw it...

RICHARD

You saw our taxes on the back of
the bitch's favourite, cloth of
gold, ribbons, Gaultier d'Aulnay?

SIMON

I saw him.

He saw not me, nor did his demon of
a horse...a caracole, paws up,
pied de boeuf, as if my hand, my
back, it would use to step up!

When I scream quarter, what is give
me?

JEHAN

Gold?

SIMON

Oui! Gold. A blow on my head from
the gold pommel of his sword and he
berates me a king of thieves!

JEHAN

What did you call him?

SIMON

Shoved my knife a full three inch
up his mare's arse and called him
bastard...*au trot!*

35

PHILIPPE
Who calls my brother, bastard?

SIMON
I do. For recent memory of him.

(*PHILIPPE throws his full goblet at SIMON's head.*)

PHILIPPE
You lie in your throat, filth!

(*SIMON ducks the goblet. Out with his dagger, calls.*)

SIMON
*A moi! Les enfants…*kill the
bastard's brother…

(*RICHARD and JEHAN and OTHERS, knives out, some
ten of them from various parts of the room rally to SIMON.*)

OMNES
A moi! Kill the ponce…
the pretty boy…*la pisseuse…*

(*PHILIPPE has drawn his sword.*)

PHILIPPE
See it?

Stand back! My tongue licks longer
than your knives – you are warned!

SIMON
We have ten blades to your one, you
die, *fleur…cul!*

PHILIPPE
I warn. Stand back.

RICHARD
Kill the silly little prick.

(*ALL form a circle around PHILIPPE. Each calls in turn:
'Here! Here! Monsieur!' PHILIPPE thrusts his sword as
they cry, thrusts and the man steps back, another calls 'Here!'
and PHILIPPE thrusts then at him, who steps back; the
others a closing circle of knives – closer and closer.*)

(*Enter BURIDAN, richly dressed, mail, a surcoat with arms of two nude women* affronte in fess *all enclosed in a coronet about their waists, gold spurs, a sable trimmed cape. He tosses the cape onto a table and draws his sword.*)

BURIDAN

Brisons là! Enough! Five too many
for one gentleman...one...two...
three and – *à moi, à moi, messire!*

(*He wades into them, disdaining to use other than the flat of his sword on their backs, until they break and PHILIPPE and BURIDAN stand, swords on guard, shoulder to shoulder.*)

PHILIPPE

Messire?

BURIDAN

Messire?

(*They thrust together, one sword point at the neck of SIMON, another at the neck of RICHARD: both transfixed in terror. JEHAN, the OTHERS flee.*)

SIMON

Help us! You cowards!

RICHARD

Murder!

(*SIMON and RICHARD drop knives, await their fate.*)

BURIDAN

Orsini!

(*ORSINI appears.*)

These two deserve they should be
hanged.
(*To SIMON and RICHARD.*)
Do you not?

SIMON

Oui.

RICHARD

Oui.

BURIDAN

Stand as sentinels, still, while
Orsini raises the alarm...
(*To ORSINI.*)
You can fetch wine.
(*To SIMON and RICHARD.*)
What say you?

(*Exit ORSINI.*)

SIMON

Nothing. Naught.

RICHARD

Naught. Nothing.

BURIDAN

Very well. I pardon you – present
you your lives intact.
(*His sword comes up.*)
Allez au vice!

(*They flee. Enter ORSINI with wine.*)

PHILIPPE

Messire! If ever you are in like
straits you may call on me.

BURIDAN

Messire, your hand?

PHILIPPE

With all my heart!

BURIDAN

It is enough.

(*They shake hands and BURIDAN toasts.*)

A votre santé, mon jeune soldat!

Are you fresh come to Paris?

PHILIPPE

Indeed. But two hours. I came to
see the Queen, her ceremonial entry
and civic welcome.

BURIDAN

Marguerite? She is not yet queen.

PHILIPPE

Oh, but will be, tomorrow, the day
after. As soon as Louis is here
from Navarre. He also enters.

BURIDAN

Where have you served?

PHILIPPE

Flanders.

BURIDAN

They fight well there.

PHILIPPE

They do. Too well.

BURIDAN

I come from Italy.

PHILIPPE

They fight well in Italy.

BURIDAN

Excellently.

PHILIPPE

I seek my fortune.

BURIDAN

I do that.
Your fortunate expectations?

PHILIPPE

My brother captains the Queen's
Guard.

BURIDAN

Ah! Gaultier d'Aulnay.

You are sure of favourite
advancement, your brother is
refused nothing.

PHILIPPE

Yes yes… I am told as much. I
have sent him message I am here.

The rabble gone, shall you honour
me with your name, sir?

BURIDAN

Which name? The name I was born
under or the name I fight under?

PHILIPPE

Which will you give me?

BURIDAN

Buridan. *Nom de guerre.* Earned in war.

PHILIPPE

Philippe d'Aulnay.

BURIDAN

That you are.

PHILIPPE

Have you anyone at court?

BURIDAN

Not one in the common court.

PHILIPPE

What have you to offer?

BURIDAN

My sword, my head and my heart.

PHILIPPE

You are a fine-looking man – you
need rely on nothing else.
(*A laugh.*)
Love and admiration languish your
lot!

BURIDAN

Perhaps. You are gentle. But I do
have more.

Like Marguerite I am from Burgundy,

I served her father Duke Robert as
his page before his assassinate
death, we were children, she and I
and…we have a secret.

PHILIPPE

Ah!

BURIDAN

A secret that may lead to my death
or…my fortune.

PHILIPPE

Oh bonne…
(*Drinking to BURIDAN.*)
…oui…bonne chance!

BURIDAN

To you also, *mon soldat!*

PHILIPPE

I have it. I am already fortunate.

I have been approached discreetly,
behalf a young and beautiful lady
who has an…interest in soldiers.
(*Shows the ring.*)
At toll of curfew on the corner of
rue Froid-Mantel tonight I am urged
give this ring to a man will ask to see it…

(*VEILED WOMAN appears.*)

The same woman!
(*Continues addressing BURIDAN.*)
I am then to follow the man…
(*Stopping again.*)
It is the same woman, I swear. See
she beckons you.

(*The VEILED WOMAN beckons from the quay.*)

(*Music.*)

VEILED WOMAN

Capitaine?

PHILIPPE

It is her. Shall you go out to her?

(*BURIDAN picks up his cloak and goes out, followed by PHILIPPE.*)

Scene 3

Quay. The banks of the Seine.

VEILED WOMAN beckons again to BURIDAN, hisses.

VEILED WOMAN

Capitaine!

BURIDAN

Ma gracieuse?

(*As PHILIPPE joins BURIDAN the VEILED WOMAN shakes her head, backs away.*)

PHILIPPE

She will not speak.

BURIDAN

Why will she not?
(*Shaking his head.*)
You will pardon my discretion?

(*BURIDAN leaves PHILIPPE and goes to the VEILED WOMAN, bends to listen while she whispers.*)

VEILED WOMAN

A beautiful lady who loves the
sword finds yours to her liking,
she wonders to herself...

(*She drops her voice so that only BURIDAN can hear. He listens some more and then exclaims:*)

BURIDAN

Am I valiant? Am I worthy of trust?
(*Indignantly.*)
I have put Italians to the sword
for twenty years – the worst
villains I have ever contended.

My sword has fleshed their women
for a like number of years – they
are the slyest, most lubricious,
lickerous and ruttish it has ever
contented.

You may tell your mistress I never
refuse a challenge, a *rendezvous* or
a combat – all I ask is that my
opponent is belted and spurred, *mia
innamorata,* young and beautiful.

VEILED WOMAN

Elle est jeune, elle est belle.

BURIDAN

Va bene. The ring...?

(*She gives him the ring.*)

VEILED WOMAN

Adieu mon capitaine; courage et plaisir!

(*Exit VEILED WOMAN.*)

PHILIPPE

A *rendezvous*?

BURIDAN

Si.

PHILIPPE

Where?

BURIDAN

The second tower of the Louvre, its
shadow.

PHILIPPE

A ring?

BURIDAN

Oui.

PHILIPPE

Show me.

BURIDAN

Here.

PHILIPPE

The same. Sorcery. Shall you go?

BURIDAN

Oui.

PHILIPPE

Sisters?

BURIDAN

Then we become brothers-in-love.
(*PHILIPPE looks off.*)

PHILIPPE

Chut!

Here is Gaultier…my only
brother.

(*Enter GAULTIER D'AULNAY.*)

GAULTIER

Philippe. It is I, Gaultier.

PHILIPPE

Brother!

GAULTIER

Your hand, brother. Yes yes, it is
really you – at last!

PHILIPPE

Oui, c'est moi!

GAULTIER

Is your love for me strong as
ever?

PHILIPPE

As ever. You are part of me.

GAULTIER

As ever. We are one.

(*They embrace. Then clasping each the other by the shoulder, grin.*)

PHILIPPE

As ever.

GAULTIER

Who is he?

PHILIPPE

A friend of but one hour who came
to my aid with sword and valour.

Some rogues chose to insult you – I
found myself beset ten to one.

(*GAULTIER salutes BURIDAN.*)

GAULTIER

Messire! Whatever you ask of
Gaultier d'Aulnay, whatever; bid
him pray at your mother's grave and
God willing he'll be there; bid him
rise up from his knees before his
mistress – then let God guard her
port for he will sail.

At your first call he will come to
you and whether you need him shed
blood or life, he will; as he now
gives his hand.

BURIDAN

Yours is a sacred love, gentlemen.

PHILIPPE

It is. It is all we have in the
world, He, for me; me, for him.

Because we were born twins without parents, a red cross on our left arms our only means of recognition.

GAULTIER

Because we were abandoned together on the cobbles of Notre Dame, *oui.*

PHILIPPE

Because we have starved together, shivered together we are rekindled, fulfilled, inspirited by each the other...*conjointement!*

GAULTIER

When he dies I shall die, and, as he came into the world a few hours before I did, I swear I shall live only those same few hours after his death...my love, and everything I have is his...

PHILIPPE

All I own is yours!

GAULTIER

Ours.

Our horse, our purse, our sword on a signal...

PHILIPPE

Our life on a word!

GAULTIER

Au revoir, capitaine.

To my quarters, Philippe...

PHILIPPE

Ah!

Someone... I am...there is someone waits for me to attend her...this night...brother.

GAULTIER

Take care, Philippe.
(*Concerned.*)
You are young, you are a stranger.

Take care brother, I would not see
your body brought out the Seine as
young men have been – a curse on
their secret slayer.

PHILIPPE

Captain? You will go?

BURIDAN

I will.

PHILIPPE

I must, I have given my word.

GAULTIER

Our word is sacred, yes.
(*A shrug.*)
It's done, given. But tomorrow,
tomorrow morning, when the Queen
rises you must attend her court,
brother...?

PHILIPPE

Oui. All is well.

(*GAULTIER worried, turns to BURIDAN, his hand out.*)

GAULTIER

Messire, go well.

BURIDAN

Merci.

(*The sound of the curfew. Enter ORSINI. To close his doors, shutters, take down his vine leaves.*)

ORSINI

That is the curfew, *messeigneurs.*

BURIDAN

Adieu! I'm for the Louvre.

(*Exit BURIDAN.*)

PHILIPPE
Me, rue Froid-Mantel.

(Exit PHILIPPE.)

GAULTIER
I have duty at the Palace.

(*Exit GAULTIER.*)

(*ORSINI left. The curfew still ringing.*)

ORSINI
Me…the Tower of Nesle!
(*Evil laughter.*)

(*Exit ORSINI, his laughter becoming diabolical music.*)

Scene 4

Streets of Paris. Night.

It rains. A young MAN is led through the wet darkness, his eyes bandaged, then another, unmistakable shape of BURIDAN, eyes bandaged, then PHILIPPE, the same. Thunder, lightning, music of laughter.

Scene 5

The Tower of Nesle. Night.

Discovered, ORSINI at a window of the Petit Tower of Nesle.

ORSINI
It is the most beautiful
night for an orgy!
(*Closing shutters.*)
The sky is black, rain
tumbles, the city sleeps and our
river swells, laps up for its feed
of corpses…a perfect time for

love; outside, the thump and crack
of thunder; inside – a sibilance of
skin, kisses, whispers, slip of
silk, tink of glass; an outlandish
conjunction of God and Satan – a
sea simmers, little pink fish, in
and out, in and out...

(*Laughter heard from the taller tower.*)

Laugh then, young fools.
(*Yawning.*)
Me, I wait; you have an hour left to
live – me, an hour left to wait as I
waited last night and tomorrow and
tomorrow and tomorrow. What nice
malignancy! Inexorable fate!

Young eyes have seen what they
should not, lips have sucked where
they should not – sucked and been
sucked, seeing and not seeing.

Those eyes shall be put out,
those lips sealed until the day
they howl their accusations before
the throne of God!

What misfortune!

Misfortune a hundred times merited
by these imprudent gallants who
prick to the call of a night of
'*l'amour*' are hustled, engorged,
through storm thunder and lashing
flood, their eyes bandaged, their
steps prescribed, simply that they
might utter the words: '*je t'aime*',
to three spoiled women, young,
beautiful, drunk on lust, wine and
their own voluptuousness.

They can never have presumed there
was no price to pay?

There is…and I wait as a
landlord waits, to exact it.

(*Outside the call of the WATCH is heard:* 'Il est deux heures
la pluie tombe, tout est tranquille. Parisiens dormez.'
ORSINI shrugs.)

(*Enter LANDRY, the shambling one-eyed sergeant, in his
footless hose, filthy white coif, disgruntled.*)

LANDRY

Maître!

ORSINI

Che c'e ora?

LANDRY

It is two in the morning, you heard
the watch?

ORSINI

I did. Day is a long time off.

LANDRY

The others fret…

ORSINI

Zut! They get pay.

LANDRY

If I might be bold, they are paid
to kill not to wait. If they wait
they ought have a double sum – so
much for boredom – so much for
slaughtering.

ORSINI

Hold thy tongue, Landry.

Someone comes. Go! *Muoviti,
cammina!*

LANDRY
I will go, but what you tell me is
without...justice.

(*Exit LANDRY even more disgruntled.*)

(*Enter MARGUERITE, imperious, ravishingly beautiful,
suffused with passion, deshabille.*)

MARGUERITE
Orsini!

ORSINI
Madame!

MARGUERITE
The men?

ORSINI
Ready. Night flees.

MARGUERITE
Is it so late?

ORSINI
The storm drops.

MARGUERITE
Hark! Thunder.

ORSINI
Day beckons.

MARGUERITE
No no, Orsini, it is again
darkening...oh!

(*A flash of lightning.*)

ORSINI
Madame, the lights must be doused,
cushions, beds...your boat waits
to take you home and we are left
our work as usual...

MARGUERITE
But it is not as usual, this night,

this young man is not and the night
is not.

He is like to another, above all
others, do you not see it, Orsini?

ORSINI
Like to who?

MARGUERITE
Gaultier d'Aulnay. As I look up at
him, listen to him, I see Gaultier,
hear my Gaultier.

This is a boy all full of love and
passion.

What danger can he be to me or to
you, this child?

ORSINI
A plaything – not a child – to be
taken and then dashed to pieces as
the others have been.

This boy, the more you did enjoy
his bawls – the more you have to fear.
(*Urgently.*)
It is nigh three o'clock. Leave him.

MARGUERITE
No, he's mine. Others may do as
they please. This young man is mine
to save.

I never dropped my mask. Should he
see me tomorrow he would not know
my face.

He must be returned to the city
safely, sound. See to it, Orsini.

I grant it. So be it. He will live
to remember this night, burn with
the memory, heavenly dreams of love

which come but once to us on this
earth, for him, and I wish, for me.

ORSINI

Signora.

MARGUERITE

Oui. Save him. Put up your knives,
open the doors, but hurry...

(*Exit ORSINI.*)

(*PHILIPPE is heard off: 'My love, my life, my angel, what is
your name?' MARGUERITE puts her mask back on. Enter
PHILIPPE.*)

PHILIPPE

I must call you by your name!

MARGUERITE

It is day.

PHILIPPE

Day, night is of no matter, torches
flare, wine sparkles, hearts beat
and time passes. Come again, again.

MARGUERITE

No no, no more...we must part.

PHILIPPE

Part! I may never see you again.
That would be despair. We belong
one to the other! Part the links
of a chain and it is in pieces.

MARGUERITE

You promised me you would resign
to parting...it is time, my husband
will wake and look for me...it is
already light.

PHILIPPE

No no, that is the moon's light, it
slips through the clouds as I slip,
we slip...again, again.

Your husband sleeps the sleep of
the old, close to death the closer
to the day.

Again, again, an hour, then *adieu!*

MARGUERITE

No! Not an hour, not an instant. I
beg you...go!

At once, without a backward glance
never to say a word to anyone, not
even your dearest friend...

Go, from Paris, from me, now. *Now*!

PHILIPPE

Eh bien.
Oui. But...your name? Tell me.
It will sound in my ears eternal,
it will be written on my heart.

Your name? I wish to sing it ever
coming in my dreams – I know you to
be noble, beautiful and divine!

Oh, give me your colours, that I
might bear them on my lance?

I came to you at your wish but I
have looked for you for ever!

Cry your name and kiss me gone, let
me die, your favour on my helm.

MARGUERITE

Non. The night is over, all is done
and you are free, as I am free.

We are not bound to each other, not
you to me nor I to you. Obey me if
you love me, obey me if you do not.
(*Coldly.*) I am a woman, in my house. I order
you from me, out of it. Go!

PHILIPPE

I petition and you scoff, I plead
and you whip me from you.

Very well, I shall go. *Adieu.*

MARGUERITE

Oui!

(*To her gasp of relief, PHILIPPE turns to go and then plucking a pin from her coif, scratches her cheek.*)

PHILIPPE

Now I shall know you!

MARGUERITE

Oh!

PHILIPPE

Keep your name in your breast.

This bloody badge on your cheek
will tell me, next we meet, you,
are…my love!

MARGUERITE

Oh you fool.
(*Wearily aside.*)
He has wound me and killed himself.

(*Exit MARGUERITE to shriek of eldritch music. The light goes with her. PHILIPPE left alone in the darkness. Doors slam throughout the Towers. Feet scurry up stone steps, a scuffle and a cry. PHILIPPE gasps in fear as a hand touches his shoulder.*)

PHILIPPE

Qui est là!

BURIDAN

Moi.

PHILIPPE

Buridan!

BURIDAN

Oui. Do you know where we are?

PHILIPPE

No.

BURIDAN

Non. Aaaaagh, these ripe women.
(*Spits – wipes.*)
Do you know who they are?

PHILIPPE

No, I have no name, I saw no face.

BURIDAN

No, you did not...no...

PHILIPPE

What is it excites you, you tremble
with fear, no not fear, rage...?

BURIDAN

Anger, such anger. These women are
the highest in the land, you saw,
you felt that, hands pale and soft.

Have you felt before such hands on
your body – not the chap and chafe
and jerking hands of siege sluts,
garrison whores – such cold smile?

What rich clothes they shed to take
us in – her voice so soft enticing,
eyes such guile.

We are brought in the night by an
old veiled woman who drips sweet
words...noble ladies, she tells
us they are noble ladies!

Oh they *are* noble ladies!

Brought a'stumble, wet, blinded – a
dazzling place, the perfume stench
and warmth is heady – they embrace
us and with a thousand tender
caresses, give themselves without
restraint or delay, at once...

At once, open!

Open...to strangers, draggled,
dirty, drenched wet from the storm.

Yet they are the noblest of women!

At table – and we both know this to
be true – at table, they are
shameless, oblivious to everything
that is not lust or gratification.

Carried away by fumes of wine, the
rank liquor of concupiscence they
scream blasphemies, hold strange
obscene discourse, utter disgusting
words, forget all propriety, all
decency, forget the world, forget
the sky...!

For they are great and noble women
they are the highest in the land,
they are – *grandes dames très grandes dames!*
(*Bitterly.*)
Ça ira! It goes on.

PHILIPPE

So?

BURIDAN

So? Are you not afraid?

PHILIPPE

Afraid yes, but of what...?

BURIDAN

The care they take to hide their
discovering.

PHILIPPE

What care? I shall know mine do I
see her tomorrow.

BURIDAN

You saw her?

PHILIPPE

No, but with this gold pin from her
coif I cut her face.

BURIDAN

Now we are dead.

PHILIPPE

What?

(*BURIDAN shoves him to the window. Through the shutter
crack.*)

BURIDAN

There, what do you see?

PHILIPPE

The Louvre.

BURIDAN

There, below, what swirls?

PHILIPPE

The Seine.

BURIDAN

The walls which keep us are of the
Tower of Nesle.

PHILIPPE

The Tower of Nesle!

BURIDAN

Under which so many corpses are
found.

PHILIPPE

And we are unmanned!

Did you slack your sword? They
disarmed me of mine.

BURIDAN

Of what use swords now? Our only
hope is flight. The door...?

(*PHILIPPE tries it, kicks with his foot.*)

PHILIPPE

Shut tight.

Mon Dieu. Hear me…my friend, if
I am slain you must take revenge.

BURIDAN

I swear it, and if I am killed, you
must avenge my mortal fate.

PHILIPPE

I swear it.

BURIDAN

Your brother Gaultier, he has
power, to him, tell him that you
seek to avenge me. I will do the
same, you dead, but from me he will
demand proof…write it…

PHILIPPE

No pen, no ink, no parchment.

BURIDAN

We must write it!

Here in this my order tablet, you
have the pin, you have veins, write
in blood, write now, write: 'I was
killed by…'

I will uncover her, I will post her
name…she is of the court…

(*PHILIPPE writes in blood: 'I was killed by…'*)

We must flee from here our separate
ways, the better we might escape.

PHILIPPE

I from where I came, the other
tower – I will avenge you, Buridan.

BURIDAN

Very well, Philippe.

(*He takes the pin.*)

PHILIPPE

Adieu.

BURIDAN

Adieu. In life and death we are
one.

(*They embrace.*)

(*Exit PHILIPPE up the tall tower steps.*)

(*BURIDAN tugs at the door, then at the shutters of the
window. Back to the door which is thrust open by LANDRY.*)

LANDRY

Say some prayers, young man.

BURIDAN

I know that pikeman voice. Landry!

LANDRY

Buridan! Captain…?

(*A shout. Then blood-curdling cries: 'Murder! Murder!'*)

BURIDAN

Landry. For the love of heaven save
me – we have fought together.

They seek to kill me also.

LANDRY

I am sent to.

BURIDAN

Who is that? Who cries 'Murder!'?

LANDRY

They are cutting his throat.

BURIDAN

The staircase?

LANDRY

Leads nowhere…

BURIDAN

The window?

LANDRY
Can you swim?

BURIDAN
Yes.

LANDRY
There is no other way…
(*Tugging open the shutters.*)
Dieu vous garde, capitaine!

BURIDAN
(*Looks down, hastily crosses himself.*)
'Dieu, ayez pitie de moi!'

(*He leaps from the window. Splash heard.*)

(*Enter ORSINI. He has heard the splash, asks of LANDRY.*)

ORSINI
Oui?

LANDRY
Dead. In the river.

(*A crash and a stumble.*)

(*Enter PHILIPPE backwards into the room from the staircase, blood streaming from wounds in his chest.*)

(*Enter MARGUERITE pursuing him. In her hand a bloody knife. PHILIPPE turns, down on his knees.*)

PHILIPPE
*Au secours! Au secours! Mon
frère, à moi, mon frère!*

MARGUERITE
Look then, and die!

(*Standing behind him she removes her mask, tugs his head round so that he might see her face. He gasps:*)

PHILIPPE
Marguerite, Queen of France!

(*She cuts his throat and he dies.*)

Scene 6

Private apartments of the Queen in the Louvre. Day.

MARGUERITE is asleep on her bed. The sound of birds, shafts of sunlight through curtains. She lies in sumptuousness.

Music.

Enter GAULTIER through a secret door. He approaches bed on tip-toe, sits at the head, asks softly:

GAULTIER

Have the angels of heaven given you
peace as you sleep, golden dreams,
my queen? Have they my thanks?

(MARGUERITE still in daze of slumber, smiles, her eyes still closed, stretches.)

MARGUERITE

I have slept and I have seen in my
sleep a young man very like you,
Gaultier, your eyes, your voice, your
delicacies of love...
(She sits up.)
...but, I felt pain...here.

GAULTIER

You have a scratch on your cheek.

MARGUERITE

Yes, I feel it.
(Aside.)
Oh! *je me rapelle...*
(To him.)
I remember, a pin from my coif
rolled down the pillow...aaah!

(GAULTIER touches her cheek gently.)

GAULTIER

Let me see...yes...take care of

your beauty Marguerite, it is not
just yours, it is mine as well…

MARGUERITE
It was not you in my dream, it was
your shadow, your mirroring.

GAULTIER
Then it was my brother spoke to
you, my other person, half my life,
my very second…love.

MARGUERITE
And the first…?

GAULTIER
You. You are hope, life, existence,
I live through you. I count the
beat of my heart in the beat of
yours, a touch is enough. Could I
but enter your body as you live in
mine…kiss your soul…?

MARGUERITE
No sweet friend, my dear, no, let
me have your pure love, for a queen
lives in fear of indiscretion, one
sneer is enough to bring her death.

Suffocate between two rude pallets
will be my fate, but you…he will
castrate.

Take heart that I love you as you
love me and never fail to say you
do…words of love like music.

GAULTIER
Tomorrow he comes, the music dies.

MARGUERITE
Your King. He comes to claim his
throne farewell trysts, farewell

long sweet meanderings, farewell
liberty – he comes to claim his
city, his crown, his land and me.

Can you still see the scar?

GAULTIER
Yes.

(*Fanfare. Noise.*)

MARGUERITE
So late!

GAULTIER
Yes, you must dress…

(*He starts to go, an order tablet drops from his sleeve.*)

MARGUERITE
Pick it up, go…no, let me see…

(*She reaches for it. He laughs, holds it from her, above her at
the reaches.*)

GAULTIER
No no…

MARGUERITE
Yes, let me see it…what is it?

GAULTIER
An order tablet, give me at my duty
post this morning by a Franciscan,
it comes from a man I met with my
brother.
(*Holds it from her.*)
Philippe, shall you receive him?

MARGUERITE
Your brother? Present him this
morning.
(*Reaching again.*)
Let me see…is it poems, essays
of love?

(*GAULTIER evades her, still laughing, slipping the book into his sleeve again.*)

GAULTIER
No, not, I know not for am sworn
on Christ's cross by the holy old
man not to open it for two days.
(*He shrugs.*)
My brother's friend, mine become,
fears misfortune.
(*Smiles.*)
Should it happen to him I am sworn
I must open it. I must go.

MARGUERITE
I shall see it.

GAULTIER
The court hastens to your rising. I
must be seen impatient with them.

MARGUERITE
Yes yes, but not of them for you
are my lord, my real lord my true
master, my king, for who else
reigns if love rules? *Au revoir.*

GAULTIER
Yet...?

MARGUERITE
Go! You must...

(*She draws the last curtain of her bed, but thrusts out her hand as she calls: 'Charlotte! Charlotte!'*)

(*GAULTIER kisses her hand and exits through secret door.*)

(*Enter CHARLOTTE.*)

CHARLOTTE
Madame?

(*MARGUERITE gestures with her hand then withdraws it.*)

MARGUERITE

Faites ouvrir les appartements.

CHARLOTTE

Faites ouvrir les appartements!

(*The call goes up throughout the palace. Trumpets, drums.*)

Scene 7

The corridors of the Palace. Day

CHAMBERLAINS, GUARDS, ATTENDANTS open drapes, curtains, doors, shutters and sunlight streams in. They call: 'Faites ouvrir les appartements! La Reine! La Reine!'

Enter COURTIERS, PIERREFONDS, SAVOISY, RAOUL then GAULTIER. They form their groups of interest – chaperon hats, wide-sleeved garnache cloaks of splendid silks, velvets.

SAVOISY

Ah, Gaultier, you got here betimes.
As ever.

GAULTIER

No no...

SAVOISY

How does the Queen rise?
(*Declaiming.*)
How does Marguerite, of France,
Burgundy and of Navarre rise,
this sun-blest day?

GAULTIER

Messire, how can I know?

Salut, messieurs, salut!

Does my brother ask for me? What
news of the night?

SAVOISY

The King sends flags, heralds, will
enter the city tomorrow and Messire

de Marigny orders the people must
cry: *'Noel!'* along the route...
Until then, they cry: *'Malediction'*
along the banks of the Seine.

GAULTIER

Why?

SAVOISY

Another young man dead, one wearies
of fishing them out.

DE PIERREFONDS

They damn de Marigny for it. So
they should. He is give charge of
our safety. He vaunts his power.
(*Dropping his voice.*)
The more corpses the better if we
can bury him under them.

GAULTIER

(*To another group of COURTIERS.*)
I expect my brother, *messieurs*...

DE PIERREFONDS

Should the King not take care he
will lose a good third of his
noblest and richest subjects, all
of them fine young men I am told.

But what possesses them to choose
drowning? To go off so, like they
are kittens or worth no thought?

SAVOISY

Seigneur, surely you do not believe
they take particular care to float
dorsum, weed choked, in the Seine?

DE PIERREFONDS

Are they led to it by demons, Jack
o' Lanterns?

SAVOISY

Rivers are not most secret places
for bodies to lie – a watery grave
is soon sunk but sooner seen. Water
floats up what the earth eats.

There are many houses from Saint
Paul to the Louvre bathe their feet
in the Seine, open their windows to
the ooze...

RAOUL

The Tower of Nesle.

SAVOISY

Oui. I passed it at two o'clock
this morning, ablaze with light.
I loathe that great black double
thrust of stone which sprouts at
night into a malevolent spirit,
tumescent over the city. Fire
flares from it like from the black
lungs of Hell; black it thrusts,
silent black, under black sky, the
river boiling at its feet...

There are revolting stories.

GAULTIER

Seigneur, you talk of a royal
residence!

(*Enter DE MARIGNY.*)

SAVOISY

I do. Enough. The King rides in
tomorrow, and the King, as you all
know cares naught for news of any
body but his own.
(*Seeing DE MARIGNY.*)
Is that not so...monsigneur de
Marigny?

DE MARIGNY
Messieurs, first tell me what you
said – that I might give proper
patience to your question.

SAVOISY
We applauded that the people of
Paris were a people most happy to
have Louis the Tenth for king and
in ecstasy to have you monsieur de
Marigny for first minister of the
Treasury...what condign bliss!

DE MARIGNY
They would not fare half so well
did they have you first anything,
monsieur de Savoisy!

(*A shout off:* 'La reine, messeigneurs!' *taken up by*
GAULTIER.)

GAULTIER
La reine, messeigneurs.

(*Enter MARGUERITE.*)

MARGUERITE
Dieu vous garde, messiers.

Scene 8

The Queen's Morning Progress.

She walks, with her GUARD and LORDS, through the corridors and
audience chambers of the palace, the courtyards, the gardens. Way
cleared by GUARDS, swept by courtesy, salutes and curtsies of
LADIES and GENTLEMEN of the Court. Fanfares. Anthems.

MARGUERITE
Ask what you will of me – what
favour, what justice – for tomorrow
I give way to Louis, my lord,
my master, the King.

69

*(She talks on the move rarely pausing, attended by
CHARLOTTE. The PETITIONERS follow, some prostrate
themselves, are ignored.)*

SAVOISY

Not so, madame!

You remain our Queen, by blood, by
beauty a true ruler of France; as
long as our King, God protect him,
has eyes and a heart.

MARGUERITE

Bravo! vous me flattez, compte.

*(The tight group round her consists of SAVOISY,
PIERREFONDS, DE MARIGNY, GAULTIER, RAOUL.)*

Seigneur Gaultier, where hide you
your brother that he might put de
Savoisy's blandishments to shame?

GAULTIER

I confess to anxiety, madame. He is
not here, though I had his word...

*(They pass a NECROMANCER once, then again.
NECROMANCER looks hard at CHARLOTTE, her face.)*

(Music. PIERREFONDS regards him aghast.)

DE PIERREFONDS

The necromancer, see him?

SAVOISY

Oui. Is he brought by de Marigny
that he might the better cast his
spell on us?

DE PIERREFONDS

See how he looks at the ladies, at
each face as if to burn brands on
them with his eyes.

Paris seethes with sorcery, every
step one takes may be the last for

gypsies, witches, necromancers,
their curses and their magic – what
else is it brings young men to a
drowned death?

GAULTIER
It is sad truth – another body this
morning below the Tower of Nesle.

DE MARIGNY
Two.

MARGUERITE
(*Aside.*)
Two?

DE PIERREFONDS
They need blood for their witchery.

SAVOISY
Not water?

DE MARIGNY
It is evil work of more substance
than fetid conjurings.

MARGUERITE
Monsieur de Marigny who would have
us all bewitched by him the better
to order our ways, does not believe
in necromancy, he tells us our fate
and how he will tax for it.

SAVOISY
Throttle for it, at end of his
magisterial rope for it, tried,
taxed and dangled taut. Wizardry.

DE PIERREFONDS
What else can be cause except it is
gypsies, witches and necromancers?

There is one there…
(*Turns – points.*) Gone, he's gone!

> MARGUERITE
> Summon him back, that he might tell
> us future things, such as what the
> King may announce to monsieur de Marigny
> tomorrow. Have him fetched.

(*Exit SAVOISY to look for NECROMANCER. His shout heard off: 'Come here, gypsy, the Queen needs good news!'*)

> DE PIERREFONDS
> That they need blood is true, foul
> secrets only yield to disgusting
> profanities.

(*Enter SAVOISY, bemused, he laughs, shrugs.*)

> SAVOISY
> He comes, but where he went when
> coming I know not…

> DE PIERREFONDS
> Aaaah! His science is give him by
> either God or Satan – we do well to
> protect ourselves.

(*He makes sign of cross, all except DE MARIGNY join him.*)

Scene 9

The Throne Room. Day.

The NECROMANCER appears, unseen by all but DE MARIGNY who goes aside to him.

> DE MARIGNY
> Sorcerer, if you wish a welcome in
> this company proclaim a thousand
> scandals rather than merely one, a
> thousand deaths, not one, and know
> that however you may excite the
> others I shall hear you calmly and
> with complete disbelief – now spin.

NECROMANCER
Make your atonement with God. You
have three more days of life.

(*SAVOISY exclaims in laughter, seeing him:*)

SAVOISY
He passeth through walls!

DE MARIGNY
I thank you – there are none know
with certainty they have…three
hours to live.

(*The NECROMANCER sweeps his arm, points, resting on GAULTIER, SAVOISY reacting in mock horror as the finger passes over.*)

NECROMANCER
You sir? You are Gaultier d'Aulnay
and you wait your brother but…he
does not come.

GAULTIER
Where is he?

NECROMANCER
They throng the banks of the Seine.

GAULTIER
My brother!

NECROMANCER
They surround two bodies and cry
out *'Malediction!'*

GAULTIER
My brother!

NECROMANCER
One. Go down to the river.

GAULTIER
My brother!

NECROMANCER

See the left arm of one of the
drowned then cry: *'Malediction!'*

GAULTIER

My brother! My brother!

(*Exit GAULTIER precipitantly. SAVOISY comments drily:*)

SAVOISY

Lo! He sees what others have seen
but as they passeth not through
walls have not come yet to tell us.

(*COURTIERS follow to watch GAULTIER go.
MARGUERITE standing motionless, the smile of dismissal
fixed on her face and becomes a grimace, the finger of the
NECROMANCER pointing at her, pale, her cheek with its
red scratch towards him. He says quietly:*)

NECROMANCER

Marguerite de Bourgogne!

Is royal destiny beyond divination.
Can mere mortal not see, not read?

(*COURTIERS turn back, their laughter freezing at sight of
the QUEEN, her pale anger and fear. They mutter: 'The
Queen! Is she witched?' The mood has changed to discomfiture.*)

MARGUERITE

I wish to know nothing, nothing.

(*DE MARIGNY at her side, hand on sword, solid, dependable
and MARGUERITE clutches at him, then flees to her throne
as if for sanctuary.*)

NECROMANCER

And yet you would have me come, me
here, Marguerite…you must now
heed what I tell you.

MARGUERITE

Do not withdraw, monsieur de
Marigny.

(*Her hand out to DE MARIGNY again.*)

NECROMANCER

Oh Marguerite Marguerite! why
must your nights be darkest black
without...warm bright within?

MARGUERITE

Who fetched this gypsy? Who asked
for him? What does he want of me?

(*NECROMANCER has reached the throne, foot on the steps.*)

NECROMANCER

Marguerite, is there not, by your
count, one body less? Did you not
believe, this morning, there would
be three bodies and not two?

MARGUERITE

Say no more, unless it is what
gives you this power of divination.

NECROMANCER

Here is my talisman, Marguerite.
(*The pin.*)
Ah! Your hand flies to your cheek.
(*Aside.*) It is she!
(*Aloud.*) Very well, I have more to say, but
to you alone, madame.
(*To DE MARIGNY.*)
Leave us, seigneur de Marigny.

DE MARIGNY

I shall not. I take orders from
none but the Queen...

MARGUERITE

Then take them, and go.
(*To the COURT.*)
Go! Leave! Go!

(Leaving DE MARIGNY, MARGUERITE comes down from the throne, takes the NECROMANCER aside, he whispers urgently:)

NECROMANCER
Your love, your honour, your very
life is in my hands.

MARGUERITE
Yes yes…

NECROMANCER
At curfew tonight I shall wait for
you at Orsini's tavern.

MARGUERITE
No, a Queen of France cannot…

NECROMANCER
It is no distance, it wants but a
bolt flight from…
(Raising his voice.)
…the Tower of Nesle.

MARGUERITE
I shall come, I shall come.

NECROMANCER
Bring, parchment and the Seal.

MARGUERITE
I will. So be it.

NECROMANCER
Go back, shut up your apartments to
all.

MARGUERITE
To all?

NECROMANCER
Most above all, Gaultier d'Aulnay.
(Going.)
Messeigneurs, the Queen commends
you to God!
(To MARGUERITE.)

A ce soir, chez Orsini, Marguerite.

MARGUERITE
A ce soir.

(*Exit MARGUERITE in haste. Shouts. Doors close throughout the palace:* 'Fermez les appartements! Fermez…!')

(*Exit the NECROMANCER / BURIDAN, the COURTIERS reeling back from him as he goes.*)

DE PIERREFONDS
Is this man not Satan, himself?

SAVOISY
Monsieur de Marigny?

DE PIERREFONDS
What was said?

SAVOISY
Monsieur?

DE MARIGNY
I heard, messieurs but I remember
only that which concerns me.

SAVOISY
Oui?

DE PIERREFONDS
Will you not henceforth take heed?

DE MARIGNY
Why now, when I would not before?
He predicted disgrace, I am still
in office; he predicts my death
and, by the living God, messieurs,
if you need assurance that I am
alive and well, say so, I have a
sword will speak for me!

(*A cry off: 'Justice!'*)

(*Enter GAULTIER, distraught.*)

GAULTIER

Justice! My brother, messeigneurs,
my brother Philippe, my only
friend, my only kinsman, throat
cut, drowned, dragged up on the
banks of that accursed river... I
demand justice, I demand his killer
that I may chew from him his neck,
set my feet on his foul carcase...
(*Accusing DE MARIGNY.*)
You, *messire*, you must answer to me
for this! On you it sits! You
guard our city, noble blood shed is
blood smeared on your honour...

SAVOISY

Gaultier, my friend...

(*GAULTIER throws himself at the doors to the QUEEN's apartments.*)

GAULTIER

I have no friend. I had a brother I
have no more, I must have him live
or his murderer dead. Marguerite!
(*Hammering on the doors.*)
Marguerite!

(*GUARDS and DE MARIGNY pull him from the doors. He draws his sword. A half circle of GUARDS, DE MARIGNY, SAVOISY around him, their swords drawn.*)

DE MARIGNY

Stand, hold, young man!

SAVOISY

Gaultier!

(*GAULTIER launches himself at them. DE MARIGNY defends the doors from his frenzied assault, the GUARDS reel back, one injured, SAVOISY scratches GAULTIER at the shoulder, another GUARD beats down his sword and GAULTIER sobs:*)

GAULTIER
I demand justice of the Queen!

(*Exit GAULTIER, bloody and distraught.*)

Scene 10

Streets. River. Gate Saint Honoré. Night.

Toll of Curfew. MARGUERITE, veiled, cloaked against night. Recognition sweeps through the emptying streets and miasma of the river towards the Gate of Saint Honoré. Music. Behind her, unseen by her, follows GAULTIER. Loud knocking.

Scene 11

ORSINI's Tavern. Night.

A small, dark smoke-filled room, with fire, some furniture but not much, rushes on the floor.

Enter ORSINI, bowing low.

ORSINI
House and master, signora, command
me and mine.

(*Enter MARGUERITE uncovering her face.*)

MARGUERITE
I want nothing but your quittance.

ORSINI
Signora I am gone.

MARGUERITE
Stay.
(*Listens.*)
I am alone and at this hour.

ORSINI
Alone and at this hour.

MARGUERITE

Which is strange.

(*Listens.*)

That which makes me come alone and
at this hour is strange...

(*A knock.*)

...also. A knock?

ORSINI

A knock. That door.

(*He points.*)

MARGUERITE

I shall open it. Your quittance.

ORSINI

I am gone. *Volatilizzarsi!*

MARGUERITE

Silent, on your life.

ORSINI

I am deaf, I am without a tongue
but if you need me I shall hear.

(*Another knock.*)

MARGUERITE

I will attend it.

(*Exit ORSINI.*)

BURIDAN

(*Speaking off.*)

Open the door, Marguerite.

MARGUERITE

Is it you, necromancer?

BURIDAN

It is.

(*MARGUERITE opens the door and recoils in fear. Enter
BURIDAN, in half mail, leather jerkin, sword and dagger,
a red painted sallet.*)

MARGUERITE

You are not the gypsy...?

BURIDAN

No, by God, I am Christian, was,
have been, faith only lives with
hope, I have been without both.

(*He sits. MARGUERITE says coldly through her fear:*)

MARGUERITE

I expect you to uncover and stand.

BURIDAN

I shall do so.
(*Stands – removes sallet.*)
Not for you are a queen, but that
you are a woman. There is no queen
here, see these smoked walls, this
floor, its straw...is there here
any trinket, asset, chattel of a queen?

Queen, where are your guards? See,
where is your throne?

Here is a woman trembles hot and
pallid in anger and fear and a man
is cold as ice.

I am crowned king for my demeanour.

MARGUERITE

Who are you?

BURIDAN

You know my name which was.

MARGUERITE

I do not.

BURIDAN

Now it is Buridan.

MARGUERITE

I know it not.

BURIDAN

You are afraid. Your guards drag
chains in the Seine – for what do they
look?

They look for another body.

They look for me.

MARGUERITE

C'est impossible!

BURIDAN

Impossible?

In the Tower of Nesle were three
noble ladies, their names the
highest in the land, the princess
Jeanne, the princess Blanche, and
the Queen, Marguerite.

With them were Hector de Chevreuse,
Philippe d'Aulnay, and Buridan the
captain from Burgundy. Me.

MARGUERITE

Burgundy?

BURIDAN

Oui, Burgundy.

MARGUERITE

They are dead, you live.

BURIDAN

I live. Gaultier d'Aulnay lives, swears to
avenge his brother. He the one who
scratched your cheek.

MARGUERITE

The Queen loves Gaultier d'Aulnay,
he her.
(*Scorn.*)
You will speak to Gaultier d'Aulnay
and tell him that the Queen killed
his brother?

You are a fool Buridan. You will
not be believed.

Now that I have your secret as you
have mine it needs only a sign from
me for you, Buridan, captain, from
Burgundy to be poled down where you
stand.

BURIDAN

It needs more.

It needs a notes book and what is
writ within it, in blood, which
blood there was plenty before you
opened his neck.

Gaultier d'Aulnay has the last
blood writ words of his brother and
he is sworn fast, by a priest of
St Francis he will read them should
I not stand before him, tomorrow at
ten o'clock.

I, Buridan, captain, who saw
scratched in fear and rage, 'I was
killed by Marguerite de Bourgogne'...
with a gold pin, from your coif.

This pin.

There is as well a second secret.

Marguerite, anatomise, dig into my
heart with twenty poignards and you
will not exhume this second secret.
Have me slid into the Seine to
embrace again the shades of my
companions of the night, Philippe,
poor shrieking Hector, my secret
will float upon the surface and
tomorrow at stroke of ten,
Gaultier, my avenger, will cry out
for an accounting, demand blood

price for his brother and for
me. 'I shall come from the knees of
my mistress,' he said, in oath
to me! Am I a fool?

MARGUERITE
If this is so.

BURIDAN
It is so.

MARGUERITE
What will I give you...let you
plunge your hands into my treasure
for gold, the specie of the state;
or the death of an enemy perhaps?
(*The Seal.*)
Here is the Seal, parchment, you
said I had to bring...are you
ambitious? I can give you whatever
chain of State you wish...

Speak. What?

BURIDAN
All, and more.

Listen to my words Marguerite.
Here we stand, not king or queen
you and I but man and woman bound
by pact we cannot sunder but by
death of one or other – on pain of
malison.

MARGUERITE
What? Speak.

BURIDAN
Marguerite, I want sufficient gold
to pave a palace.

MARGUERITE
You shall have it. I shall melt
down sceptre and crown that you do.

BURIDAN

I would be first minister.

MARGUERITE

De Marigny is that.

BURIDAN

I want his title and place.

MARGUERITE

Not but by his death.

BURIDAN

I want his title and place.

MARGUERITE

You shall.

BURIDAN

You are left your lover and your secret.

We two will reign, the State and France ours to dispose.

We two stand one, king and true king and, I guard my lips for ever.

You shall have a boat, moored each night, on the river. Those windows of the palace look out on the Tower of Nesle will be blinded.

Acceptes-tu, Marguerite?

MARGUERITE

J'accepte.

BURIDAN

You accept that tomorrow at this hour I shall be first minister of the Treasury?

MARGUERITE

You will be.

BURIDAN

Tomorrow at ten I shall come to the
court for the little book, my order
tablet, with which I have sent men
their glory.

MARGUERITE

You will be received.

BURIDAN

Now, write an arrest for de
Marigny.

(*MARGUERITE writes and signs the order for DE MARIGNY's
arrest, affixing the Seal.*)

MARGUERITE

Here.

(*BURIDAN takes the parchment.*)

BURIDAN

C'est bien, adieu Marguerite, à demain!

(*Exit BURIDAN.*)

MARGUERITE

(*Spits her rage*)
'A demain, démon!'

Fiend! Devil!

God will need help you if the day
comes I have you in my hands as you
have me this night!

(*Going.*) Foul, foul fortune follow you who
dare defy me.

Me, a great duke's daughter!

Me, the wife of a king!

Me, me, me, regent of France!

(*Exit MARGUERITE into the night. Music.*)

Scene 12

The banks of the Seine at Saint-Honoré. Night.

MARGUERITE hurrying back to the Louvre, stops and rages yet again:

MARGUERITE
That cursed book! I offer half my
blood to he who brings it me.

GAULTIER
(*Off.*)
Marguerite!

(*Enter GAULTIER.*)

GAULTIER
Marguerite, *c'est toi?*

MARGUERITE
Gaultier!
(*Aside.*)
He is come to me.
(*Turning on him.*)
Faithless wretch...what do you
here?

GAULTIER
(*Taken aback at her apparent anger.*)
I followed you. I seek justice.

MARGUERITE
Justice? Ask me for justice? Give
me that book hides your guilt.

GAULTIER
I have no guilt. I would find my
brother's guilty murderer.

MARGUERITE
Your brother dead will be avenged,
his slayer found – I swear it. Now

give me that which is close to your
heart, some other love confided.

GAULTIER
I have no other love.

MARGUERITE
Then you have no justice given you.

GAULTIER
Marguerite, I must have justice.

MARGUERITE
Must? There is no justice except
of the crown and that not easily
bought – except, that love may
sway. Give me the book, see justice
flower, on kisses – who loves?

GAULTIER
None but you.

MARGUERITE
You lie.

GAULTIER
You are the repository of all my
love, all I have left now, more,
for my brother gone...there is
more.

MARGUERITE
You lie. Let me feel your heart,
what beat it makes can prove your
innocence or no...justice there.

(*She leans against him. Feels his breast.*)

GAULTIER
What do I lie?

MARGUERITE
Your loves. You have a book I'm told, some
words, some songs, a *juec d'amor*,
you are a troubador and ladies of

the court have heard you sing from
it, their names within it...

GAULTIER

They lie, they lie. I have no
skills of love song, none...

MARGUERITE

You have and here is proof.

(*She plucks the notebook from his sleeve.*)

GAULTIER

Oh no! I am sworn, you must not
have it.

MARGUERITE

What are you sworn?
(*Scorn.*) What am I sworn? Have I never
broke oath for you? Forget I am
forsworn for you, for treachery in
love is more than in the
adulteress, forget and keep your
word...
(*Giving him back the notebook.*)
...and, me, I keep my jealousy.

Justice done, forgot. *Adieu!*

GAULTIER

Marguerite, in heaven's name, keep
me my honour!

MARGUERITE

Honour! The honour of a man!

The honour of a woman, is that then
nothing? You have sworn?

But, me; one word, one thought of
you and I have forgot my oath made
before God.

And I would forget it again, and
again and again, and did you pray

me do so, I would forget the entire
world for you!

(*He holds out to her the notebook.*)

GAULTIER

Mon Dieu, pardonnez-moi!
(*Not letting go.*)
Is it angels or demons urge me
forget my brother, my oath, my
honour...?

(*He gives it her in agony of indecision. She takes it and walks
from him, saying calmly, aside:*)

MARGUERITE

I have it.

GAULTIER

Forgive me, my brother. I fear that
I, though I know not how, forswear
thee this night.

(*MARGUERITE surreptitiously tears a page from the book
and comes back to GAULTIER, to give it him.*)

MARGUERITE

It was a madness. There is nothing in
the book.

My Gaultier does not lie.
(*They embrace.*)
You shall have your justice.

The name of your brother's murderer
is known to me.

GAULTIER

His name?

MARGUERITE

He comes to court tomorrow where
you will arrest him.

GAULTIER

His damned name?

MARGUERITE

Precede me to the palace where an
order will be put out for his
arrest, and you shall yourself
arrest him...take care you will?

(*She leads him off, then lets him precede her.*)

GAULTIER

I shall, I shall! *Merci, merci, ma
reine...*
(*Going – off.*) ...his name?

(*MARGUERITE with the small piece of paper, loiters to say
aside:*)

MARGUERITE

Oh! Buridan, it is now me holds
your life in my hands!

(*Exit MARGUERITE.*)

(*The rain starts to fall. Music. The WATCH is heard:* 'Il est
deux heures, la pluie tombe, tout est tranquille. Parisiens
dormez.')

Scene 13

At front of the Louvre.

*Bright morning, bird song. Music. Discovered RICHARD, looking at
the river. Gates of the Louvre closed. An ARBALÉTRIER in his
pepperpot in a corner of the wall. A balcony.*

*Enter SIMON. He joins RICHARD and looks up at the
ARBALÉTRIER and contemplates the river with RICHARD.*

SIMON

C'est toi, Richard?

RICHARD

Oui, c'est moi, Simon.

(*They contemplate the river some more.*)

SIMON

You fish?

RICHARD

Non.
(*Another sigh.*)
I look for them.

SIMON

Fish?

RICHARD

They go to the devil the highest in
the land and, by water, rather than
by land.

SIMON

Oui. And what do you do here, nose
in the water, back to the palace?

RICHARD

I watch the foot of the Tower of
Nesle for any noble fish on his way
to the devil with his throat cut,
that I might offer him *bon voyage.*

SIMON

None?

RICHARD

None.

(*Another sigh. SIMON then brightens, asks:*)

SIMON

Are they all gone?

RICHARD

Oui!

(*Enter SAVOISY.*)

(*RICHARD turning to go comes face to face with him.*)

SAVOISY

Get into the gutter, idiot!

RICHARD

Oui, monseigneur...
(*Quickly doffing.*)
No, they are not all gone, Simon.

SAVOISY

You speak?

RICHARD / SIMON

We pray God will you preserve...

SAVOISY

Very well.

RICHARD

¦...from going to the devil.

SIMON

...by land.

(*Exit RICHARD.*)

(*Exit SIMON.*)

(*Enter SAVOISY's page OLIVIER to tell him:*)

OLIVIER

The gate is closed, monseigneur.

SAVOISY

No, Olivier. It is nine o'clock.

OLIVIER

No, monseigneur, it is tight shut.

(*Enter RAOUL with his PAGE who goes before.*)

SAVOISY

What is this, Raoul?

RAOUL

What?

SAVOISY

The Louvre closed?

RAOUL

Wait. They will open.

SAVOISY

It is a fine morning. Walk with me.

RAOUL

Arbalétrier!

ARBALÉTRIER

Monseigneur?

RAOUL

Know why the gate is not open?

ARBALÉTRIER

Non, monseigneur.

SAVOISY / RAOUL

Non?

(*Enter DE PIERREFONDS.*)

DE PIERREFONDS

Salut, messires.

It appears the Queen holds court
from her balcony this morning.

SAVOISY

Ah, you divine it so…
(*Crossing himself.*)
…seigneur de Pierrefonds! *Oui!*

(*Enter BURIDAN, impressive, with five MEN-at-ARMS.*)

BURIDAN

Stay here!

SAVOISY

Excite your divine gift more. Who
is this fresh come with a half
lance of men; a *conducteur,* a *chef
d'escadre,* judge and executioner to
rival de Marigny, marquis, duke?

DE PIERREFONDS

I know him not.
Perhaps some Italian *condottiere,*
seeks his fortune.

SAVOISY

Seek? This *fanfaron* will seize.

(*BURIDAN contemplates them, nods.*)

BURIDAN

And will hold what he seizes.
(*Another nod.*)
Messeigneurs.

(*SAVOISY, DE PIERREFONDS, RAOUL huddle.*)

DE PIERREFONDS

I hear that Belial voice!

RAOUL / SAVOISY

Moi aussi!

(*SAVOISY sees off.*)

SAVOISY

Seigneur de Marigny comes, to mount
Christian guard with us!

(*Enter DE MARIGNY.*)

DE MARIGNY

Why do you not enter the palace?

BURIDAN

I will tell you, monseigneur.
An arrest is to be made. The palace
is closed to asylum.

DE MARIGNY

Arrest? I know not of an arrest!

BURIDAN

Here, monseigneur.
(*The parchment and Seal.*)
For your improvement: read.

SAVOISY

Farewell compliment, things
complicate...

DE MARIGNY

Give it me.

BURIDAN

Read it loud.

DE MARIGNY

'By this order of Marguerite, Queen
reigning and regent of France, that
Buridan, captain of Burgundy shall
arrest, seize hold Enguerrand de
Marigny, where found.'

BURIDAN

C'est moi. Buridan, captain of
Burgundy.

DE MARIGNY

By the Queen's ordering?

BURIDAN

Your sword!

DE MARIGNY

Take it from its scabbard. It is
without stain.
(*The sword.*)
When the hangman kicks me, soul
from body, it will fly up pure as
my sword.

BURIDAN

To the Chateau Vincennes!

DE MARIGNY

From there?

BURIDAN

Montfaucon will serve.
Where you took care erect a gibbet,
their inspiration there, it is but
just you try it.

DE MARIGNY

Captain, it was erect for criminals
not martyrs.

(*Crosses himself.*) Thy will be done.

SAVOISY

Eh bien! Next it will be sorcery
captivates him.

DE PIERREFONDS

Abracadabra! The gates open!

(*Enter GAULTIER with five ARBALÉTRIERS.*)

SAVOISY

To let out, not in.

GAULTIER

Are you Buridan?

(*BURIDAN greets GAULTIER with a friendly nod.*)

BURIDAN

You know me Gaultier. I am before
you, safe and well.

GAULTIER

You, who stood with my brother…

BURIDAN

I did. It is ten o'clock, have you the
book I gave you?

GAULTIER

…are suspect and accused of his
murder.

BURIDAN

Ah!
(*Laughs.*) It is me she will have?

GAULTIER

It was you took him to his death.
(*The warrant.*) Read. Read it loud.

BURIDAN

'By this order of Marguerite, Queen
reigning and regent of France, that
Gaultier d'Aulnay shall arrest…'

Are you not come to me on your oath

97

Gaultier, give to a priest of Saint
Francis? It is ten o'clock.

GAULTIER
Your sword!

BURIDAN
My order book!

GAULTIER
Your book?

BURIDAN
Oui, do you not have it?
(*Given the book.*)

I would have taken it from you as
we agreed but now there is that
which must...
(*Holding it – elated.*)
...be said before you arrest me.

(*BURIDAN opening the book.*)

SAVOISY
We arrest the world today!

(*BURIDAN with the note book open, his elation turning to
consternation.*)

BURIDAN
Gaultier! From this book a page is
torn...

GAULTIER
Then it is so.

BURIDAN
Who?

GAULTIER
Who?

(*He looks up at the balcony in confusion. MARGUERITE is
not there.*)

BURIDAN

My blood is on your head.

GAULTIER

Me?

BURIDAN

Look. See, a page ripped out!

What was writ, Gaultier?

GAULTIER

I know not.
(*Again up at the balcony.*)

BURIDAN

Marguerite! You gave it the Queen.

GAULTIER

I admit I did.

BURIDAN

So. *Eh bien.*

(*Enter MARGUERITE on balcony.*)

GAULTIER

What was written?

BURIDAN

It is gone.

GAULTIER

What?

MARGUERITE

Remove that man to the prison,
grand Chatelet!

GAULTIER

What was written?

BURIDAN

Gone. Written in your brother's
blood, signed by your brother,
written by your brother...

MARGUERITE

Take him off!

GAULTIER

What? Tell me…

BURIDAN

It said: 'Gaultier d'Aulnay is a
man without faith, without honour.
He cannot keep for one day that
which is give him in trust to his
honour and his faith!'

(*To GAULTIER in scorn.*)
There you have it, what it said,
faithless gentleman.
(*To MARGUERITE.*)
Salut! Marguerite!

(*With DE MARIGNY's sword BURIDAN salutes
MARGUERITE. GAULTIER wary, steps back drawing his
own sword. BURIDAN turns to the young man and goes on
guard. GAULTIER thrusts at BURIDAN who parries with
the prime Parade and disarms him neatly by taking the young
man's sword under his left arm in a Disarm on the Carte.
This done, looking at the ARBALÉTRIERS who have raised
their crossbows, BURIDAN tosses both swords at GAULTIER
to catch and presents his own sword, first offering it to
MARGUERITE.*)

BURIDAN

Marguerite! To you the first pass,
a parry and a disarm, but to me the
counter thrust *en revanche,* I hope.
(*To the ARBALÉTRIERS.*)
Messiers.

(*Exit BURIDAN with GAULTIER and escort.*)

(*Exit MARGUERITE from the balcony.*)

(*CHAMBERLAINS, GUARDS, ATTENDANTS open the
gates, the windows, the doors of the palace. They call:* 'Faites

ouvrir les appartements! La Reine! La Reine!' *SAVOISY shakes his head in confusion.*)

SAVOISY

Messeigneurs. We had best attend
the Queen!

(*Exeunt OMNES. Music.*)

(*Curtain.*)

ACT TWO

Music. The sound of twelve iron bound doors clanging shut, chains, groans. The curtain rises.

Scene 1

A dungeon in the prison grand Chatelet. Night.

Darkness. When light comes a chimney of slime-encrusted stone is seen going up and up, stone steps spiralling. Far above there is a tiny grating through which ordure drips and sometimes flows. BURIDAN discovered, alone, bound, lying on the ground – he twists and thrashes and arches up in his bonds – under the chimney. He whispers hoarsely:

> BURIDAN
> A man took hold tight my hand,
> whispered *'courage'*.
> (*He calls.*)
> Are you there? Who were you?
> (*Echoes.*)
> I know him not, could not see him.
> (*Calls.*)
> Who are you?
> (*Echo.*)
> It is enough, the heart leaps, a
> friend! There is a friend will
> bring fresh water, fresh bread, a
> priest at my death, for death it
> will be, soon, she cannot let me
> live, will not...
> (*Calls.*)
> Who are you?
> (*Echo.*)
> Down the steps, one hundred and
> twenty, twelve doors slammed...
> (*Calls.*)
> *Allons!*

(*Echo – he shouts in anger, twisting.*)
…*allons!* Buridan! *Allons!*
(*Angrily.*)
You have an account with Satan long
and intricate, set it right in your
mind, your conscience…insane!
(*Calls.*)
Insanity!
(*Echo.*)
I know the honour of men.

Men shriek honour and turn and run,
men sob honour while it pumps from
them with their blood.

Man's honour, like glass, shatters
at the compliant laugh; like snow,
it melts in the heat of a woman.
(*Calls.*)
Insane! I have suspended my life
on such a gossamer thread as man's
honour…insane insane insane
insane insane insane insane, a
hundred times, a thousand times,
insaaaaaaaaaaaaaaane!
(*Echo echo echo.*)
How she mocks, in the arms of that
faithless perfidious abject knave
Gaultier…. Gaultieeeeeeer! Each
kiss snatched from him should tear
her heart, his heart reproach,
remorse, compunction, sorrow!

Whilst I…me…me, I roll and
rail and struggle, bound, on cold
stone, earth, under the soil, in
this tomb…
(*Roars.*)
Insane! I should have stretched
him, laid him, struck him down and
removed him from out this world.

(*Laugh.*)

It is possible!

(*A glim of light up high.*)

I see a single star in a dark sky,
just one to guide me, despairing
traveller that I am. She. She.

She will want to see and, insult my
death with her presence – that is
the star I see.

You demons who sculpt the hearts of
women with mallet and chisel, I beg
you have not left ungraved that
perversity of sentiment I augurate
will have her come...the Queen.

(*Anguish – the light out.*)

Oh it is a little star and it is
gone *out*!

(*Fury.*)

Out! Out! Out!

Who were you?

(*The echoes, creak of a door opening.*)

(*Chink of light again now near and on the level of BURIDAN.
The huge bulk of LANDRY fills the doorway.*)

(*Enter LANDRY. He whispers, dimming the light:*)

LANDRY

Capitaine, où êtes vous?

BURIDAN

Ici. Qui va là!

LANDRY

C'est moi. Ami.

BURIDAN

Qui, toi? I cannot see.

LANDRY

A friend need not be seen to be
known!

BURIDAN

Landry, again you come, I am saved!

LANDRY

Impossible!

BURIDAN

What do you here then?

LANDRY

I am a gaoler.

BURIDAN

Gaoler here, assassin at the Tour
de Nesle... what employment!

LANDRY

Oui, enough.

BURIDAN

Durst thou do nothing? Shall you not
get me my priest?

LANDRY

No, but I can hear your confession,
and give it word for word to your
priest; and, what penance he gives,
word as a soldier...it, I shall
as well do for you, every word.

BURIDAN

Imbécile! Something to write upon?

LANDRY

Impossible!

BURIDAN

My purse.

LANDRY

Oui.

BURIDAN

Here, this pocket...
(*A purse.*)
Spill it out. Count it. How much is
given you as gaoler?

LANDRY

Six livres a year. *Parisis!*

BURIDAN

Count the gold while I consider.

(*LANDRY counts.*)

Have you counted it?

LANDRY

Have you considered?

BURIDAN

Oui, how much?

LANDRY

Three gold marcs.

BURIDAN

One hundred and sixty-five livres.

LANDRY

Parisis?

BURIDAN

Tournois. But that is twenty-eight
years' labour in this prison.

Swear to me on your hope for heaven
you will do what I prescribe and
this sum is for you. It is all. Had
I more, it would be more.

LANDRY

Et vous?

BURIDAN

If they hang me, which is likely,
the hangman will pay for my cold
interring and I shall not need it

but, if I save myself you will have
four times as much…and, me, a
thousand times.

LANDRY

What?

BURIDAN

Go to my lodgings, my room, shut
yourself secret within, count the
stones from the corner where you
see a crucifix stand.

(*LANDRY crosses himself.*)

On the seventh stone, a cross.

(*Crosses himself again.*)

Your dagger, prise it up. In sand,
you will find a small iron box, the
key to it in this purse, open
it…you may assure yourself it
contains only papers, not gold.

If tomorrow when the King comes to
Paris you see me not safe, sound,
and saying to you 'Give me the box
and the key', you will, down on
your knees give both, to Louis and,
if I am dead I am thus revenged.

That is all; my soul will rest, it
will be to you I owe thanks and the
bitch will smother!

LANDRY

You may place your trust in me.

BURIDAN

On your eternal soul?

LANDRY

On it as I hope for paradise, I do
swear.

BURIDAN

Adieu, Landry. Try to be an honest
man.

LANDRY

I shall try, *capitaine.*
(*Going then coming back.*)
Mais…mais c'est bien difficile.

(*Exit LANDRY. The light is taken up by LANDRY, and the
twelve doors slam.*)

BURIDAN

Allons! allons! Come hangman,
come noose, vengeance is crouched
at the foot of the tree.

Vengeance! A word, merry, sublime
from living lips, deep sonorous and
empty from the grave and which, no
matter how loud it re-echoes…

(*Calls.*) Echo-echo-echo!
(*Echo echo echo.*)

…can never wake the corpse
laid in a tomb…

(*Calls.*) I am tombed!
(*Echo.*)

(*A small and secret door opens silently from another cell.
Enter MARGUERITE. ORSINI waits in the cell.*)

ORSINI

Attento…!

MARGUERITE

Is he bound?

ORSINI

Tight. Limb to limb and chain to
stone.

(*BURIDAN sees the light.*)

BURIDAN

Qui va là?

MARGUERITE

Orsini, wait. Should I cry – come
with lance straight for his heart.

(*Hand out.*) The knife!

BURIDAN

Qui va là?

(*ORSINI gives her a knife, goes back into the cell to watch
and wait.*)

MARGUERITE

C'est moi!

(*BURIDAN utters a deep sigh 'Aaaaaaaaaaaaaaagh'.*)

BURIDAN

You are come.

Lantern lit you seek shivering
pleasure still, my death, in
glorious, voluptuous certainty of
your triumph.

Oh wanton woman, oh epicurean
woman, *à moi! à moi!* here to me!

MARGUERITE

No prayer you utter will melt my
heart…

BURIDAN

I utter none, none…

MARGUERITE

…in vain…

BURIDAN

…but I excite you more.

MARGUERITE

…love, Buridan, lodged deep in a
young man's heart will gnaw corrode

those other puerilities honour,
faith, oaths of loyalty – sworn to.

Love diseases. You foolish put your
trust in a man sick of it from his
scalp to his scrotum.
(*A lantern.*)
You would have him read this piece
of paper 'I die assassinate by the
hand of Marguerite...'
(*The paper.*)
See! See! Look! Death...
(*She burns it.*)
...last flames, last hope! Am I
free now, Buridan?

You are arrest for the murder of
Philippe d'Aulnay...not I.

BURIDAN
But I know a secret.

MARGUERITE
There are poisons of such terrible
violence they shatter their phials,
such are your secrets, take care of
your heart...which contains them.

Who will you tell?

BURIDAN
Marguerite, come closer your body.
I will tell.

MARGUERITE
Too late, I am gone.

BURIDAN
I shall wail your name at my
trial...

MARGUERITE
Trial? No trial for a man like you
...a priest...

BURIDAN

...moan your name at my hanging.

MARGUERITE

Hanging? No hangman for you...
a priest...and a bully for you,
the priest starts it, the bully
ends it here, this dirty place,
here your last place on earth,
where the walls deaden anguish, put
out sobs, choke cries, here is
where you will convulse your
last...strangled by your own hand
– ever known to be incontrovertible
proof of guilt.

BURIDAN

Then shall I whisper my secret to
myself...if you come close you
might hear it, if you go you will
not and...you will wonder.

(*MARGUERITE going.*)

(*BURIDAN whispers and she stops, not sure what she has
heard. ORSINI comes out. MARGUERITE turns her back,
closes the door on ORSINI. She stands by the door and the
whispers of BURIDAN stay whispers but become louder, and
louder and more seductive, she curves her body towards him
and hears:*)

BURIDAN

... Duke Robert, of Burgundy...a
beautiful young daughter – her body
that of an angel, her soul that of a
demon...her name...

(*The whispers fade.*)

(*MARGUERITE whispers also:*)

MARGUERITE

Her name...?

BURIDAN

…a page with a heart frank and
open and trusting…

MARGUERITE

Her name…?

BURIDAN

…whose name was Lyonnet de
Bournonville… and they loved.

It is a strange story, they loved
but none knew, each night he came
and each morning he went…
(*He groans.*)
I am… I am…help me to change
round to the other side to lie. I
am in such pain this side…
(*She does.*)
…*merci, merci*…
(*He smiles his thanks.*)
She told him in tears, Lyonnet de
Bournonville, that she was with
child, in her womb, Marguerite.

And her father the Duke sped her to
a convent, Marguerite.

But first a last tryst of tears,
before the doors of the convent
closed for ever, as if her tomb,
Marguerite.

For her, to be her tomb.

Oh, this was a hideous night, they
clung and they cried and looked at
a…dagger and they…

Please! Please…these ropes…

MARGUERITE

What did they do?

BURIDAN

...bite my flesh and pain, such
pain.

A dagger.

She held it like you hold that
knife, and she said 'Lyonnet, Lyonnet,
if this time tomorrow my father...'
(*Groans.*)
Pity, I beg you, cut these ropes.

(*On impulse MARGUERITE cuts the rope which binds his
arms and BURIDAN gives a sigh and a laugh and says no
more.*)

MARGUERITE

What more?

(*BURIDAN looks at her, says nothing. She bends over him
and laughing softly, BURIDAN continues:*)

BURIDAN

'...if tomorrow my father is
dead, there need be no convent,
no parting, only love, our love...'

The dagger passed from her hands to
the hands of the page. In the dark
his arm taken and, like led through
the paths of hell...a hand lifts
a curtain...the page armed, the
duke asleep.

The noble head of the old man, calm
asleep and serene, seen so for ever
by his assassin page, in his dreams
and in his waking hours for ever,
in infamy...for ever...

Marguerite, the young and beautiful
Marguerite, entered not a convent,
not she... Queen of Navarre, Queen
of France – she!

MARGUERITE
Me.

BURIDAN
You.

Next day, by hand of one Orsini,
the page had a letter sent him, and
gold. Marguerite bid him hence for
ever – after their vile crime they
must never meet again.

MARGUERITE
A letter, how imprudent.

BURIDAN
A girl she was then, would not now.

Some last compunction, some guilt
of conscience had her set it down
in all its shocking complicity and,
in her hand and, her name.

MARGUERITE
He went, did he not, Lyonnet de
Bournonville, never to be seen
again, he and the letter lost?
How may this concern a queen?

BURIDAN
You know how it may.

The letter will be the first
petition of Louis the Tenth of
France, his entry into Paris,
tomorrow.

You gloat me what the punishment is
for murderers Marguerite, now hear
how a parricide and an adulteress
will die.

Hair is shaved with red hot shears.
They are opened, living, for to

draw the heart out, which is burnt,
cinders flung to the wind.

Three days after, the mutilate body
is took through Paris on a hurdle.

MARGUERITE

Grâce! grâce!

BURIDAN

These ropes, my hands, another
service you may do...my hands.
(*She cuts ropes.*)
Fetch in priest and bully, here is
the garrot!
(*The rope.*)
And tomorrow the cry 'Buridan,
murderer of Philippe d'Aulnay
strangled in prison!'

Another cry heard answer from the
Louvre: 'Marguerite de Bourgogne is
to die for adultery and parricide.'

MARGUERITE

Have pity Buridan...

BURIDAN

I am Buridan no more!
(*Cries.*)
I am Lyonnet de Bournonville,
Marguerite's page, the killer of
Robert of Burgundy – his master,
and her noble father!

MARGUERITE

You cry out! You will be heard.

BURIDAN

What do you fear? These slimed
walls deaden anguish, put out sobs,
choke cries...

MARGUERITE

What is to be done?

BURIDAN

Again?

MARGUERITE

Oui...what?

BURIDAN

You ride tomorrow on the right of
the King, I shall ride on his left.

MARGUERITE

So be it. I shudder but say it.

BURIDAN

C'est bien.

MARGUERITE

The letter?

BURIDAN

When the letter is offered the King
I take it, as his first minister.

MARGUERITE

De Marigny is not yet dead.

BURIDAN

You swore...

MARGUERITE

He has an hour to live.

BURIDAN

Eh bien.
(*Stopping her going.*)
Wait. The child?

MARGUERITE

Child? Chi... I gave to a man.

BURIDAN

His name?

MARGUERITE

I forget.

BURIDAN

Think Marguerite, and you will
remember.

MARGUERITE

Landry, I think. Orsini? A man.

BURIDAN

Landry! Landry!

MARGUERITE

What do you do?

BURIDAN

Orsini!

MARGUERITE

He is not…

(*Enter ORSINI.*)

BURIDAN

Orsini.

MARGUERITE

…here.

BURIDAN

Approach Orsini. I am first
minister of France.

Assure him, Marguerite.

MARGUERITE

It is true, he is first minister.

ORSINI

Command me, *maresciallo.*

BURIDAN

The lamp, a star to light us…
(*To MARGUERITE.*)
Take my arm, madame.

MARGUERITE
Where do we go?

BURIDAN
To meet before our King, Louis the
Tenth in triumphal entry to Paris.

Alla luce delle stelle…!

(*Exeunt OMNES, the doors open to keys and clang, all twelve
of them.*)

(*Music.*)

Scene 2

The banks of the River Seine. Day.

*Double tower of the Tour de Nesle, a hidden quay and steps up from
the river. City wall. Gate of Saint-Honoré. Boats.*

*Heard off. Fanfare. Drums, trumpets, bagpipes and cymbals. A clamour
of horse, foot, shout: 'Noel! Noel!' that is the triumphal entry of
KING LOUIS X into Paris. Horses, lances, banners shadows across
the scene. Crescendo of noise and then fading.*

Scene 3

Private apartments of the Queen in the Louvre. Day.

*MARGUERITE appears to be asleep on her bed. Music. Sound of
birds, shafts of sunlight through curtains. She lies in sumptuousness.*

*Enter GAULTIER through a secret door. He approaches the bed, on
tip-toe, sits at the head, speaks very softly, gently and sadly:*

GAULTIER
Oh my queen, how I longed the night
through my duty, for sun to rise,
to break, to warm the morning so
that I might wake you softly, with
my love, this last time…my

brother gone now none but you, what
consolation I have is you…

CHARLOTTE

Seigneur!

(*CHARLOTTE sits up on the bed. GAULTIER bewildered.*)

GAULTIER

Where sleeps the Queen?

CHARLOTTE

Has she not returned?
(*Off the bed.*)
That she has not or I would not be
here, in her bed…

She took her cloak I gave her, last
night, but where I know not…

She left me wait and, wearying of
her return, I lay upon her bed and
slept, until I heard such sweet
words, so softly spoke… I woke.

I thought I was…you woke me…
seigneur…in heaven.

(*GAULTIER is distraught.*)

GAULTIER

Not returned? How could she not
return? Where could she go that
she went the night… where has
she slept, where does she wake?

(*CHARLOTTE screams as GAULTIER draws his sword.*)

CHARLOTTE

Seigneur, I am not to blame, no,
please, your anger play elsewhere.

I know not where she went.

(*GAULTIER puts his sword up. Ashamed at his action.*)

GAULTIER

Forgive me, Charlotte, she would
once tell you, as once me, every
thing.
(*Dejection.*)
This is a dagger to my heart.
(*Angry he accuses.*)
She gave you secret where!

CHARLOTTE

Would she had, your anger has me
fear for her. What I knew I would
tell – but nothing do I know.

We are hers, and used we to know
all, but there is one knows more,
has known her since a child...

He, the Italian, Orsini, has often
secret consortation with her and is
admit when he demands, her command.

GAULTIER

Yes, he!
(*Going.*)
Open the apartments Charlotte and,
forgive me my brutality.

(*Exit GAULTIER.*)

CHARLOTTE

Bon courage, monseigneur! I pray
for you.

(*Opens the curtains, the doors, the bed.*)

(*The cry goes up:* 'Faites ouvrir les appartements! Faites
ouvrir les appartements!')

(*Doors opened in the palace, one room to another by GUARDS
and a few COURTIERS enter.*)

Scene 4

Chamber in the Louvre, balcony. Day.

Enter DE PIERREFONDS and SAVOISY.

SAVOISY

You wait not on Louis,
his triumphal entry, de Pierrefonds?

DE PIERREFONDS

No, I wait upon Marguerite, her way
shall be mine.

SAVOISY

I wait him here as well...

For there is such a great flowing
of loyal people I fear drowning –
it being in fashion – in the muddy
ooze of loyal love.

If the Queen go, I too, with you.

DE PIERREFONDS

It is just possible Savoisy, you
think the King to be the Queen, not
the King she greets...

SAVOISY

It is.

DE PIERREFONDS

It is?

SAVOISY

Just. It would be.

(*Enter RAOUL.*)

DE PIERREFONDS

Bonjour, baron. What of the King?

RAOUL

He comes, marshals, flags, banners
and pursuivant at arms before, the

Queen rides at his side…

(*Cries heard outside:* 'Vive le roi! Vive le roi!')

RAOUL
(*Continued.*) …on his right.

DE PIERREFONDS
Then we are not right placed.

SAVOISY
We left it too late.

RAOUL
At his left hand…

SAVOISY
I would be glad told, not Gaultier
d'Aulnay…!

RAOUL
Then rejoice! Not anywhere.

SAVOISY
What? Not?

Bid them drag the river messieurs
down from the Tower of Nesle, for
he is as pretty as his brother.

RAOUL
He who rides in place of Gaultier
is the Italian *condottiere,* he,
arrest by Gaultier and thrown in
the prison of grand Chatelet.

Unpunished – to my sight, not a
mark, complete with eyes, with
nose, with ears, with lights, with a
head stuck firm on shoulders out
his sweetly worn armour – not even
flogged, he.

DE PIERREFONDS
What say you to that, Savoisy?

SAVOISY

We live in very strange times. On
yesterday de Marigny was first
minister, today not, but arrested.

Likewise yesterday, the captain
arrested, today he rides where de
Marigny would ride, in complete
possession of his limbs and neck.

RAOUL

And lights.

DE PIERREFONDS

Sorcery. I declare it!

God jousts with Satan for the
Kingdom of France!

(*Cries from outside, nearer:* 'Noël! Noël! vive le roi!')

(*Enter GUARDS, MARSHALS, a POURSUIVANT at Arms
with the arms of France emblazoned to warn:*)

POURSUIVANT

Le roi, messieurs, le roi!

(*Enter LOUIS X. Music.*)

LOUIS X

Salut, messeigneurs, salut!

We are blessed with fine soldiers
fight for us in Champagne and, as I
count, many fine courtiers here.

SAVOISY

Sire, the day soldiers and court
march together against our enemies
will be a great day for France.

LOUIS X

That we might the better march
together on campaign I give order
that a tax be levied on the city of
Paris, as celebrate my entry.

(*To the balcony, a wave:* 'Vive le roi! Vive le roi!')

LOUIS X
Oui, mes enfants, I shall cut all
taxes in measure of my love for
you, *mes enfants*...subjects...my
people!

(*Enter BURIDAN and MARGUERITE.*)

BURIDAN
Remember. To we two the power, we
two are France!

(*From without:* 'Vive le roil Vive le roi!')

LOUIS X
Oui oui, mes enfants.
(*To BURIDAN.*)
De Bournonville, you will raise a
new tax from the trades and guilds
of Paris in order that this tax
will pay for the old tax I have at
a stroke abolished – one will pay
for the other and it will be just.

(*Leaving the window he says to all the Court.*)

Messeigneurs, here is my hand waits
its bathe in your kisses!

(*LOUIS X puts out his hand. SAVOISY, DE PIERREFONDS, RAOUL and other COURTIERS rush to kiss the hand of the King.*)

(*Music.*)

(*PETITIONERS are admitted. They enter and cry:* 'Vive le roi! Vive le roi!' *GUARDS hold them back in an entrance. Among them LANDRY, transfixed with awe at sight of the King. BURIDAN extricates LANDRY from the other PETITIONERS and takes him aside. LANDRY's gaze never leaves the King.*)

BURIDAN

I am here. You see.

I say to you, 'Give me the box, and
the key!'

(*LANDRY disappointed...*)

LANDRY

You are safe?

BURIDAN

Oui.

(*...but lives in hope.*)

LANDRY

You are not harmed?

BURIDAN

I am not harmed. Safe, sound and I
say to you, 'Give me box and key!'
(*A thought.*)
You have it?

LANDRY

You have the twelve marcs?

BURIDAN

Tonight.

LANDRY

Where?

BURIDAN

At my lodgings.

LANDRY

Tonight I will give it you. I will
give you the box and the key if you
are safe and...

BURIDAN

There are many things I have need
question you, many...

LANDRY
I will answer all.

BURIDAN
C'est bien.

LANDRY
I would have liked to go down on my
knees before the King.

(*Exit LANDRY reluctantly.*)

(*Enter GAULTIER, rashly approaches the Queen, whispers:*)

GAULTIER
Madame, where slept you?

MARGUERITE
Gaultier!

GAULTIER
Tell me.

MARGUERITE
Gaultier, take care!

(*GAULTIER sees BURIDAN, exclaims:*)

GAULTIER
Buridan, here?

What does he, here?

(*GAULTIER, hand on sword, prevented from reaching
BURIDAN by the Queen who whispers to him urgently, a
hand on his arm:*)

MARGUERITE
Gaultier, I love you, you alone, I
shall love you for ever!

(*He breaks free of her, pushes through the COURTIERS who
scatter, to reach BURIDAN, his sword half out of its scabbard.
MARGUERITE says loudly, so all can hear:*)

MARGUERITE
Come, captain, and kiss the hand of
the King.

(*Again.*) Come!

(*GAULTIER confused. The King, all the court looking at GAULTIER, waiting. BURIDAN lets his sword slide back. GAULTIER bows to MARGUERITE. He approaches and kisses the hand of LOUIS, who then smiles grimly at them all and says:*)

LOUIS X
Now it is time for me to rule,
messeigneurs, come those of you are
my council, come my queen, come
Lyonnet de Bournonville, the
Kingdom awaits our consocation.

(*GUARDS push back the PETITIONERS who cry:* 'Vive le roi! Vive le roi!' *POURSUIVANT at Arms commands:*)

POURSUIVANT
Place au roi!

(*A sweep of COURTIERS, GUARDS, and exit LOUIS.*)

POURSUIVANT
Place à la reine!

(*A sweep of COURTIERS and GUARDS and exit MARGUERITE.*)

POURSUIVANT
Place au premier ministre!

(*Exit BURIDAN.*)

(*Exit POURSUIVANT.*)

SAVOISY
Lyonnet de Bournonville. That is
not the name of a *condottiere!*

The name is old. It has fame.

I am awake, messeigneurs, do you
assure me?

If I am not I shall be wakened,
if I am I shall be sent off – what

ever state, I am eager to see the
finish of this thing.

Gaultier! You must know.

GAULTIER
Ask me not, messeigneurs, for I
know nothing...ask me not!

(*Enter POURSUIVANT.*)

POURSUIVANT
Le sire de Pierrefonds!

DE PIERREFONDS
Voici.

POURSUIVANT
Ordre du roi.

(*He hands DE PIERREFONDS a parchment with seal.*)

(*Exit POURSUIVANT.*)

(*DE PIERREFONDS reads, puzzled.*)

DE PIERREFONDS
It is an order I shall repair to
Vincennes, take up de Marigny our
once first minister, deliver him to
Mounfacon where, without doubt, he
will dangle from his own gibbet.
(*Regret.*)
I never wished him well.

SAVOISY
Bien! The first order in council
of our king is a death warrant.

My compliments on your commission.

DE PIERREFONDS
I would have hoped for better than,
but, what I am commanded by my King
I shall accomplish.

Adieu, messieurs.

(*Exit a troubled DE PIERREFONDS.*)

SAVOISY

Adieu...!

(*Enter POURSUIVANT with another parchment.*)

POURSUIVANT
Le compte de Savoisy?

SAVOISY

Oh, oh, *voici.*

POURSUIVANT
Lettres patentes du roi.

(*Hands him the letters patent.*)

(*Exit POURSUIVANT.*)

RAOUL

What?

SAVOISY

Oui.

(*He holds the parchment.*)

> The first order makes me reluctant
> to open the second for fear, who?
> (*Waits.*)
> If it is an order of death for one
> of us, you, it is better to delay.
> (*A deep breath.*)
> But, this king brooks none.
> (*Opens it.*)
> I am commissioned a captain of the
> guard. Is there a place?

RAOUL

None but that give Gaultier.

(*SAVOISY looks at GAULTIER who stands alone at the balcony.*)

SAVOISY
By God! I ever wished him well.

RAOUL

Nevertheless, you are congratulate.

SAVOISY

I am to safe guard the apartments.
That my task and appointment.
(*Reads.*)
At once.
(*A relieved snigger.*)
Then I durst not delay...
what it is to be favoured...
(*He laughs.*)
So know the King is a great king,
the new first minister *nonpareil!*

(*Exit SAVOISY with an embarrassed glance at GAULTIER.*)

(*Re-enter POURSUIVANT.*)

POURSUIVANT

Sire Gaultier d'Aulnay!

GAULTIER

Hein?

POURSUIVANT

Lettres patentes du roi.

GAULTIER

Not she, but from the King?

(*GAULTIER given the letters patent. POURSUIVANT addresses the rest of the COURT.*)

POURSUIVANT

Messeigneurs, the King, our lord
will not receive after the council,
you have his permit you may retire.

(*GAULTIER reading the letters patent.*)

GAULTIER

'...command of the province of
Champagne...leave Paris at once
for Troyes!'

Me? Leave Paris? Command in
Champagne…why?

RAOUL

It is a step Gaultier, you are to
be congratulate, it is fair reward
and the Queen could not equal it.

GAULTIER

Congratulate!

Then congratulate Satan, archangel
that he was, he now commands Hell!

I shall not go.

Were you not bid go? Then go. I
shall not…

(*Anger.*) *Go!* The King did bid you go!

RAOUL

God protect you, Gaultier.

(*Exit RAOUL and all the COURTIERS hurriedly, leaving
an angry GAULTIER, hand on sword, pacing, bewildered.*)

GAULTIER

Go… I shall not go, bid leave
Paris! Me? Is this what I was
promised? I was not!

The ground moves, this is not
ground I have trod these last days,
for all about me things move, that
which I have held real, even as I
touch, vanishes…phantoms!

(*Enter MARGUERITE.*)

MARGUERITE

Gaultier!

GAULTIER

It is you at last, madame!

Do you mock me that you promise and
then break your word?

Am I a child's toy – am I a child
for you to laugh at? But
yesterday you swore we would never
part, today I am hasten from Paris
to a province…!

MARGUERITE
It is not so.

GAULTIER
Not so? I have it here…how
could you?

MARGUERITE
I was forced, Gaultier.

GAULTIER
Forced! Who may force a queen?

MARGUERITE
A demon, with power.

GAULTIER
Who? Tell me…

MARGUERITE
You must seem to obey, at once,
go! Tomorrow, here, I will relate
the reasons for your banishment.

GAULTIER
You cannot expect I shall go on
such…

MARGUERITE
I can! I do.

GAULTIER
I will come back that you might
tell me better reassurance.

MARGUERITE
Oui. Return tomorrow, Gaultier.
(*Looks off.*)
Someone comes. Go, Gaultier!

GAULTIER
Remember this promise. *Adieu!*

(*Enter BURIDAN.*)

BURIDAN
Forgive me my impediment to your
adieux, Marguerite.

MARGUERITE
You are mistaken, Buridan.

BURIDAN
Was that not Gaultier left you?

MARGUERITE
We said not *adieu.*

BURIDAN
Did you not?

MARGUERITE
He is not to leave.

BURIDAN
The King orders him gone.

MARGUERITE
I order him stay.

BURIDAN
You forget our covenant.

MARGUERITE
I promised you would be first
minister, you are, you promised me
Gaultier, now you send him go!

BURIDAN
We said we two would be France, you
now say we *three,* him also.

He cannot he brought party to our
confiding.

MARGUERITE
Notwithstanding, it will be.

BURIDAN

Have you forgotten I have you still
in my power?

MARGUERITE

Oui. But then it was when you were
Buridan, my prisoner.

You now are Lyonnet de Bournonville
…of France, first minister.

Destroy me, destroy yourself.

With your life give back to you,
you have honours, rank, riches and
power and…greater height from
which to fall!

We are together on a slippery crag,
you toss me from it and you must
follow, our cries heard mingle in
our plunged destruction.

BURIDAN

You love him?

MARGUERITE

More than life.

BURIDAN

I would have thought I could stamp
on your heart, crush it, hack it,
twist it, without risk of a single
drop of human feeling.

Love? You have been brought low,
Marguerite, that you search for it.

We are rulers of France, not any
more creatures of whim and fancy,
tears have no place in our eyes,
regret no place in our hearts and
love none, not it, not affection of
any kind lest we are surrendered.

I believed you to be a demon. I now
fear you to be only a fallen angel.

MARGUERITE

I shall not let him leave my side.

BURIDAN

Not…?
(*Aside.*)
I am lost do I not destroy them
both?
(*Aloud.*)
Marguerite, if I tell you that your
love for this young man is for me
intolerable, in that it awakes me
memories of what was once our own
and; what you have seen in me as
ambition, the quest for vengeance
is…love, my love…oh if…?

And…if I tell you also, that
all that which I have gained is
only for one purpose; that we might
be as we were, the page Lyonnet and
the young Marguerite together again
as one, the letter give you back in
proof that what I now have is
naught but my desire to be once
again as we were.

If, if say, say, if, you find in me
this devotion, this love…say you
not now he must be sent, gone?

MARGUERITE

Is it true, or mockery, Lyonnet?

BURIDAN

Receive me tonight and tonight I
return you the letter but, not as
it has been, not hate, not menace,
no no, love, that love again.

Let us meet in love and tomorrow
you will have the letter and I not.

All I gain is rendered you back.

MARGUERITE
Should I...

If, if I do receive you, it cannot
be here at the palace.

BURIDAN
Can you not leave as you wish?

MARGUERITE
Where? Where might we...

BURIDAN
The Tower of Nesle?

MARGUERITE
...meet?
(*Taken aback.*)
You would meet me there?

BURIDAN
Have I not already there met you
for just such purpose, our meeting
separate only by the caprice of a
veiled woman?

MARGUERITE
(*Aside.*) He yields!
(*Aloud.*) I confess to a weakening, a strange
frailty, Lyonnet...that happiness
there was...your voice evokes
souvenirs d'amour I had thought
dead, buried...deep in my heart.

BURIDAN
Marguerite!

MARGUERITE
Lyonnet!

BURIDAN
Gaultier will go hence?

MARGUERITE
Sent tonight, do you wish it.
(*A key.*)
Here is a key will give you in by
the postern of the Tour de Nesle.
(*She gives it him.*)
I must leave.
(*Going – a last aside.*)
Ah! Buridan, this time you will
not escape.

(*Exit MARGUERITE, leaving BURIDAN with the key.*)

BURIDAN
The key to your tomb, Marguerite.

But, be assured you shall not rot
in it alone!

(*Exit BURIDAN.*)

Scene 5

A garden at the Louvre. Day.

*Hedges, trees, the sound of the river lapping. Enter SAVOISY.
BURIDAN heard off: 'Compte de Savoisy!' SAVOISY stops and
waits.*

Enter BURIDAN.

BURIDAN
Compte de Savoisy.

SAVOISY
Me voici, monseigneur.

BURIDAN
Give this to Gaultier d'Aulnay.

(*BURIDAN hands SAVOISY a note. Then holds up a warrant bearing the royal seal.*)

SAVOISY

Monseigneur.

(*SAVOISY tucks away the note.*)

BURIDAN

There is this for you.
(*The warrant.*)
The King pains to learn of the
night killings of young men,
Savoisy, which afflict the city.
He views with suspicion the Tower
of Nesle and orders you go there,
with a lance of ten men, at nine
o'clock tonight. You will seize and
detain all there found whatever
in title or rank.
(*Giving him the warrant.*)
You have your warrant here.

SAVOISY

I have seigneur, my first!

I shall not prove tardy.

BURIDAN

That is as well, Savoisy!

(*Exit SAVOISY with great self-importance.*)

BURIDAN

For it is the most important order
he will ever discharge.

(*Exit BURIDAN.*)

(*Enter MARGUERITE from the palace, towards the river, through the garden. She stops at a hedge, calls softly:*)

MARGUERITE

Orsini? Orsini!

(*ORSINI appears from the hedge.*)

ORSINI

Eccomi qua, regina!

MARGUERITE

Tonight, at the Tower, have four
armed men with you.

ORSINI

Benissimo, your orders?

MARGUERITE

Later I shall give them.

ORSINI

Signora.

(*Exit ORSINI.*)

(*Exit MARGUERITE.*)

Scene 6

The lodgings of BURIDAN. Night.

*Crucifix. The stones. One of them prised up. The small box with a
candle placed on it.*

*Discovered LANDRY sitting on the stones, with wine, a piece of
chalk, his legs out around the hole. He calculates.*

LANDRY

Twelve marcs, in gold. That is…
(*Chalking.*)
…six hundred eighteen livres,
tournois, not *parisis, tournois.*

If the Captain keeps his promise
and gives me the twelve marcs in
gold, six hundred eighteen livres,
for this box, *tournois,* for which I
would not give six sous *parisis,* I
shall heed his exhortation advice
and become an honest man – at once.

But, what, how, when I am without a
trade that is honest?

For soldier is not, for what he is
asked to do.
(*A sorrowful sigh.*)
He must kill, rape and loot to the
best of his ability – at once.
(*Brightening.*)
Ma foi! With six hundred eighteen
livres, *tournois,* I shall raise a
company, captain of it in service
of some grand seigneur.

I shall pocket all he gives me and
order my men they must get their
needs from dishonesty – at once.

That I might live honest.

Vive Dieu! That is honest. There
will be honest wine and...who is it
cares for an honest woman?

Under the cross we shall do good
works, assist those we meet with
too much gold or goods to enter the
Kingdom of heaven – where they will
get their just reward – in poverty.

At once!

Sang-Dieu! If I am not mistaken a
happy and honest life and I need
not leave my trade! We shall ever
on my strict orders carry out the
duties of Christian soldiers in
regard to sorcerers, gypsies, Jews;
and flay their skin from them, easy
as swallow a glass of wine.

(*Enter BURIDAN.*)

BURIDAN

C'est bien, Landry.

LANDRY

I am here.

BURIDAN

You drink?

LANDRY

No better companion.

BURIDAN

Gold buys wine.

LANDRY

Here is your box.

BURIDAN

Here is your twelve marcs.

LANDRY

Merci.

BURIDAN

Now, I have to meet a young man
here.

(*A crash heard off. LANDRY sniggers.*)

LANDRY

The old stairs.

BURIDAN

Let him in.

(*LANDRY goes out the door. Heard off:* 'Le capitaine
Buridan?' *BURIDAN calls:* 'Le voici'.)

(*Enter GAULTIER.*)

GAULTIER

Well?

BURIDAN

I am no longer Buridan.

I am Lyonnet de Bournonville, first
minister of Louis the Tenth.

141

GAULTIER
It matters not what title you usurp.

BURIDAN
Usurp?

Why, are you not gone to Champagne?

GAULTIER
I am ordered not, by the Queen.

BURIDAN
The Queen?

GAULTIER
Oui.

(*BURIDAN holds the box, turns the key and opens it.*)

BURIDAN
I sent for you for the oath you
took, Gaultier d'Aulnay to come to
me even from the knees of your
mistress – is it she you left?

GAULTIER
It is not.

I came to you not for that oath,
for that oath died with my brother.

BURIDAN
Yet I did him service.

GAULTIER
I came for what you promised.

BURIDAN
What was that? The name of your
brother's murderer, how de Marigny
went to his death...what?

GAULTIER
No no not that, none of that, God
will avenge my brother, God will
avenge de Marigny...her.

You promised me I might see her!

BURIDAN

So you care not for anything else?

GAULTIER

God forgive me. I want her.

BURIDAN

What use am I for that? Can you
not enter by a secret door in an
alcove…you shake. Is it rage
has you do it, or is it that this
night Marguerite, like another
night sleeps not in the Louvre?

GAULTIER

Who told you?

BURIDAN

The man with whom she passed the
night.

GAULTIER

Blasphemy! You are insane!

BURIDAN

Take care, young man, take your
hand from your sword.
(*His hand on his own.*)
Marguerite is a beautiful and
passionate woman.

Writes she to you?

GAULTIER

What need you know of that?

BURIDAN

Are her words enchanting and ardent
and passionately persuasive, is her
hand round and clear and deep cut?

GAULTIER

That you shall not know, your eyes
will never light on the sacred…

(*BURIDAN holds out a letter from the box. GAULTIER glances at it, at once recognises the hand of MARGUERITE. He gasps.*)

BURIDAN

Read: 'Your beloved friend
Marguerite.'

Oui?

GAULTIER

It is falsely done! It is
infernal.

BURIDAN

Is it not tempting – when near to
her, when she talks to you of love,
when you gently run your hand in
her long hair she lets flow undone
voluptuously about her – to cut a
tress, like this?

(*From the box, a tress of hair.*)

(*GAULTIER confused.*)

GAULTIER

It is the way she writes. It is her
hair. Stolen!

BURIDAN

Ask that of her.

GAULTIER

Where? At once!

BURIDAN

Not here, she is elsewhere.

GAULTIER

Where? This instant!

BURIDAN

She has a *rendezvous*.

GAULTIER

She has a *rendezvous* with whom?

(*Hand at sword hilt.*)
I thirst for his blood, his life!

BURIDAN

Take care.
(*Smiling – his sword.*)
If he is finished his desire for
her – and will cede you rights?

GAULTIER

Me?

BURIDAN

Oui.
(*Shrugs and yawns.*)
He tires of her, has compassion for
you and, will give you free of her.

(*GAULTIER draws his sword in rage. BURIDAN his.*)

GAULTIER

How dare you!

(*GAULTIER lunges at BURIDAN who parries, steps to the side and waits for another lunge which he parries again, and again. They fight silently, GAULTIER unable to find a way through BURIDAN's guard, until BURIDAN disarms him. BURIDAN with the tip of his sword at GAULTIER's heart, drops on one knee – eyes on GAULTIER all the time – picks up GAULTIER's sword, hands it back to him.*)

BURIDAN

Young man. Tonight you will need a
sword.

(*GAULTIER accepts the sword and BURIDAN steps back, stays on guard.*)

GAULTIER

0 mon Dieu!

(*GAULTIER sheathes his sword and BURIDAN lowers his guard.*)

BURIDAN

It is past eight o'clock and
Marguerite waits... for, Gaultier?

GAULTIER

Where is she?

BURIDAN

The Tower of Nesle.

GAULTIER

(*Going.*) *Bien...*

BURIDAN

You forget the key to postern and
inner door.

GAULTIER

Give it!

BURIDAN

One more word...or so.

GAULTIER

Speak.

BURIDAN

It is she who killed your brother.

(*GAULTIER looks at him aghast, hand flying to sword again.
BURIDAN smiles gently. GAULTIER collapses, staggers from
the room, crying.*)

GAULTIER

Oh wicked wicked...!

(*Exit GAULTIER leaving BURIDAN alone.*)

BURIDAN

C'est bien!

Go meet again, find each the other,
brother through lover.

(*Calls.*) Landry!

Landry... I know you skulk!

(*Enter LANDRY.*)

LANDRY

Capitaine. At once!

BURIDAN

First, that young man, he goes to
the Tower of Nesle, how long?

LANDRY

Does he have a boat?

BURIDAN

No.

LANDRY

Half an hour.

BURIDAN

C'est bien, the glass.

(*LANDRY gives BURIDAN the hour glass. BURIDAN turns
it, settles so that he might watch it. Yawns.*)

BURIDAN

I would talk of war in Italy.

LANDRY

Monseigneur?

BURIDAN

Drink, and talk.

LANDRY

Oui.

Bitter wars and good times. Days
passed in battle, nights in orgy.

As the cellar of the Prior of Genoa
we drank dry, to the last drop.

Such as the convent of young girls
we fucked dry to the last old nun.
(*He crosses himself.*)
Days of great joy and great sins.

BURIDAN

The day we die, our sins on scales

147

against our good deeds, I hope you
can tap it that our good deeds tip.

LANDRY

I will need know them.
(*He thinks hard.*)
I have some…of that I am sure.

BURIDAN

Search your past, sergeant. Humour
me of children…

LANDRY

Oui.

It was in Germany, a child, poor
little angel. Hope he prays for me.
(*A tear wiped.*)
We pursued Bohemians, as you know,
pagans, idolaters and infidels.

On their filthy heels, some cuts we
got, a few, and then while a
village burned I heard the sweetest
sound, a poor little pagan left to
die in the flames.

I searched about me and found some
water, and in the twinkle of an eye
baptised him Christian as the rest
of us, *c'est bon!*
(*Delight then sorrow.*)
I looked for where I might put him
safe out of the fire and God spoke;
it struck me, his parents pagan!

His baptism would go to the devil
did they come back.

I put him in his cot, and went back
to my men. The roof fell in.

BURIDAN

He perished?

LANDRY

Oui. But who was it laughed?
God laughed, because when Satan
poked in the ashes for his angel he
got his fingers burned on the hot
soul of a little Christian! *Oui?*

BURIDAN

Oui.
But tell me of a child give you by
Marguerite of Bourgogne.

LANDRY

You know of that?

BURIDAN

Tell me.

LANDRY

I will. Orsini, her creature, told
me, toss in the river like cats
are, forgive me, I did not.

I was tempted and I fell.

(*He tips the imaginary scales with his finger and laughs.*)

BURIDAN

What did you do?

LANDRY

Took them to Notre Dame and exposed
them on the cobbles, Christian.

BURIDAN

(*Shaken.*) Them?

LANDRY

Them. There were two, that they
were Christians I was sure...

BURIDAN

What became of them?

LANDRY

They were taken. In the evening
they were gone.

Poor little mites, I hope one day
to meet them again and dandle them
on my knee.

(*BURIDAN asks urgently, hoarsely:*)

BURIDAN

How will you know them?

LANDRY

A sharp knife. I cut them, deep in
the arm, Christians, with a cross.

How they screamed, but it was for
the best.

(*BURIDAN has gone cold with horror.*)

BURIDAN

Which arm?

LANDRY

The left arm, each one.

BURIDAN

My sons!

One dead, the other about to be, both,
by her and by me!
(*Shatters hour glass.*)
Landry, a boat.

I must reach the Tower of Nesle
before that young man I have sent
to his death.

Where is there a boat, who?

LANDRY

Simon, the fisherman.

BURIDAN

Then your sword, and follow me.

LANDRY

Where, *capitaine*?

BURIDAN
À la Tour de Nesle, malheureux!
(*Exit BURIDAN, followed by LANDRY.*)
(*Music.*)

Scene 7

The river Seine. Banks. Night.

BURIDAN and LANDRY in the boat. GAULTIER on the banks, through mist and the skulking denizens of Paris. Music.

Scene 8

The Tower of Nesle. Night.

Music. Discovered MARGUERITE and ORSINI. ORSINI at the window.

MARGUERITE
This man knows all we hope secret,
life, death, thine, mine, Orsini.
But I contest his will these three
days, we would be in his power.

That he prevails not is remarkable.

ORSINI
The devil tells him, is at his
orders – he knows all that we do.

MARGUERITE
With a word did he force me on my
knees like a slave.

By devil wiles he had me release
his bonds, cord by cord.

Then had he the impertinence to
demand of me – all!

All, Orsini, this night!

ORSINI

But him, none other?

MARGUERITE

But him, it is a last necessity,
but him.

ORSINI

Signora. Do but command me, I shall
be the first to order 'Kill him!'

But...dare I ask, shall I say...

MARGUERITE

What dare you?

ORSINI

In what respect do I prosper, these
nights? How? Give me gain? Did I
not...what?

(*MARGUERITE is taken aback.*)

MARGUERITE

Ah, it must be done, Orsini, you
know well it must.

You also want him dead, you would
kill yea or nay for your own peace
of mind would you not?

ORSINI

For he knows what he knows I would,
this last time – not ever again.

I tire, and I do not extravagantly
prosper.

The sins pile, but little else.
(*Piously.*)
We must try cleanse our souls for our
eternal rest, our heaven bane.

MARGUERITE

While he lives I am not Queen, not
mistress of my wealth, my treasure,
not even my life but with him dead.

(*Angry.*) I swear it you, no more of it.
(*She succumbs.*)
Not only this but I shall give you gold,
as much would buy a province.

This tower shall be rased. I shall
build a convent of its evil stones.

I shall found a community of friars
will pass their days at prayer bare
foot on the bare stones.

They will be ordered pray for me and...
(*Almost a threat.*)

...pray for you, Orsini.

I am as tired as you are of these
sordid couplings, these deaths...

(*Shocking thought.*) I fear!

The thought occurs that God is
poised to pardon me only if I do
not carry out this one last death!

ORSINI

No no, it is just, he knows all, he
is lost. How comes he?

MARGUERITE

By those stairs.

ORSINI

I shall place my men.

MARGUERITE

Listen!
(*To the window.*) What is it?

ORSINI

A boat rowed by two men.

MARGUERITE

It is him.

Go, there is no time to lose. Go!
Lock the door that I am safe from

him, he even now... may surprise us.
Go, go! Secure me in against him.

(*Exit ORSINI. The door slammed boomingly shut, the key turned.*)

Gaultier! This is he would keep us
apart.

He wanted gold I gave it, honours.
I gave them...

Did you but know how much he wishes
us apart you would pardon me his
death...

Gaultier, this man is evil, this
Lyonnet, this Buridan!

And he is being sent back to the
hell from which he came! It is he
who must bear my guilt, it is he
who made me spill so much blood!

God is just, all blame will fall on
him, and me, oh me, me!

Were I my judge, I would not dare
to expect absolution.
(*Listening at the door.*)
It has not begun, I hear nothing yet,
nothing...

(*Enter BURIDAN through the window.*)

BURIDAN
Marguerite! Marguerite! Alone!
God be praised!

MARGUERITE
À moi! À moi, Orsini!

BURIDAN
Fear nothing!

MARGUERITE
You!

BURIDAN

Marguerite, there is something you
must know...

MARGUERITE

What more will you demand of me?

BURIDAN

Nothing... see...
(*Tossing them from him.*)
... Far from me, my sword, far from
me my dagger, far from me this box,
in which are all our secrets.

Now, you may kill me, I am not
armed, I am without armour. Kill
me, take the box, burn the letter
you will find within and sleep
tranquil on my grave.

I come not to do you ill, I have
come to speak...

Oh, did you but know what I have
come to tell you!

It is that which will bring back
those days of happiness, to us,
though we are cruelly cursed...

MARGUERITE

I don't understand.

BURIDAN

Marguerite have you nothing in your
heart womanly, naught of a mother?
Is she, I have known once so pure,
now, without that which is sacred
both to God and man?

MARGUERITE

Talk to me, of purity and virtue,
you!

Satan is converted!

BURIDAN

Marguerite have you never for one
moment repented?

Answer me as you would answer God
for I can offer you happiness or
despair, I can damn you or absolve
you, I can offer heaven or hell.

Can you not confess to me all you
have suffered?

MARGUERITE

There is no priest I would dare
confess to, not one. Only to
someone bears guilt equal to mine
might I confess.

You, Buridan, you Lyonnet.

But for you that young girl would
not have killed her father, would
not have lost her sons, you alone
bear guilt with me, and to you
alone can I speak of it...

Driven by remorse I sought to sate
conscience in pleasure and blood.

None bade me stop, none bade me
remember virtue.

From the mouths of courtiers came
naught but smiles.

They whispered me I was beautiful,
the world was mine, I could by
crook of finger turn everything
upside down was it my pleasure.

Without strength of conscience to
resist came a swoon of passion,
drunken remorse, dreams a'swirl
with ghosts, sensuous...pain.

Oui.

Only to one as guilty as I am could
I tell these things.

BURIDAN
Tell me if...what...had you,
your sons?

MARGUERITE
Oh!

Then, oh I dare not, could not, not
if I...no, I dare not think of it.

But I could not keep my sons.
(*She whispers.*)
My sons. I cannot say the words
for among the ghosts haunt me night
after night, not once have they
come, they who most of all should,
and it is a delicate balanced world
that of nightmare, my misplaced
words could evoke their shadows!

BURIDAN
Marguerite, they have been close to
you.

MARGUERITE
Close?

BURIDAN
One of them, on his knees, asked
for mercy...you were there, you
heard him plead...

MARGUERITE
I...when, where?

BURIDAN
Here, this room, you.

MARGUERITE
When?

BURIDAN

He was with me, that night.

MARGUERITE

Philippe d'Aulnay. I struck! You lie!

BURIDAN

No. You struck!

MARGUERITE

I struck...him. What proof?

BURIDAN

None. The word of a villainous
sergeant...what is that?

His word, he took them, marked them
with a cross, laid them front of
Notre Dame – to die or to be taken.

MARGUERITE

If it is true...?

BURIDAN

It is true.

(*MARGUERITE looks hard at him, realises, accepts, is
overcome, horrified.*)

MARGUERITE

Vengeance de Dieu! I it was struck
him...dead.

BURIDAN

Oh bitter...and...there is another.

(*MARGUERITE groans, nods.*)

MARGUERITE

Gaultier!

BURIDAN

The lover of his mother! Taste of
this...!

MARGUERITE

No, thank God...no, by heaven's
grace not so, on my knees I thank

God... I still can call Gaultier
my son, he may call me...

BURIDAN

Is it true?

MARGUERITE

By the blood spilled here I can
swear! It was the hand of God
that reached out, a strange
love, never that of a lover, always
that of a mother...it was God...

The good God, the saviour who will
have joy and repentance come back
into my life...*mon Dieu, merci,
merci.*

(*Down on her knees she prays.*)

BURIDAN

Marguerite. Do you forgive me? Are
we no longer enemies?

MARGUERITE

No, you are the father of Gaultier,
my remaining son.

BURIDAN

Our son is he who binds us, in
terrible secrecy...what we have
done...and...

Oh you struck...

MARGUERITE

I struck...!

BURIDAN

...and...love?

MARGUERITE

Oui, oui. Love.

BURIDAN

Do you believe we can be...happy
again?

MARGUERITE
I do believe it!

BURIDAN
All we need is our son.

MARGUERITE
Our son, here with us.

BURIDAN
He comes.

MARGUERITE
Here?

BURIDAN
He has the key you gave me.

MARGUERITE
Then he comes through the postern!

BURIDAN
He does.

(*MARGUERITE screams.*)

MARGUERITE
Then he is a dead man!

For that way you were to come!

(*Cries heard off:* 'À moi! À moi! Au secours!')

BURIDAN
It is he they murder!

(*BURIDAN tries to open door. Throws himself against it.*)

MARGUERITE
The door is locked. Gaultier!
Orsini! Orsini!

(*BURIDAN hammers on door with the hilt of his sword.*)

BURIDAN
Open this door!

MARGUERITE
I have not the key.

BURIDAN
Then he is dead?

(*MARGUERITE collapses, sobs.*)

MARGUERITE
He is...dead. Our son.

BURIDAN
The door opens!

(*Enter GAULTIER covered in blood.*)

GAULTIER
Marguerite... I give you back the
key to the Tower...

MARGUERITE
Gaultier, I am your mother.

GAULTIER
My mother? My mother?

(*Horror – his hand and arm out to curse her.*)

Then be damned!

(*GAULTIER dies.*)

(*BURIDAN down on knees, tugs at the dead man's sleeve.*)

BURIDAN
His arm, Landry marked his arm.

Oui. It is there, the mark of the
cross.

Our sons damned in the womb of
their mother!

A murder at their birth, a murder
cut down their life.

MARGUERITE
Pity, pity!

(*Enter ORSINI.*)

(*Enter SAVOISY with the GUARDS. ORSINI denounces.*)

ORSINI

Monseigneur. Here are they who are
the real murderers, they, not I.

SAVOISY

You are my prisoners.

BURIDAN / MARGUERITE

Prisoners? We?

MARGUERITE

I, the Queen?

BURIDAN

I, first minister?

SAVOISY

I see here no queen, no minister.

There is the murdered body of my
friend.

There two assassins.

Here an order signed by the King to
arrest this night all found in the
Tower of Nesle, whatever rank or
title!

BURIDAN

Commend me to God!

MARGUERITE

Amen, His mercy.

(*Flames of Hell lick. Consume them.*)

(*Music.*)

(*Curtain.*)

RUY BLAS

Characters

RUY BLAS

DON SALLUSTO DE BAZAN

DON CESAR DE BAZAN

DON GURITAN

MARQUESS OF BASTO

MARQUESS OF SANTA CRUZ

COUNT OF ALBA

DON MANUEL ARIAS

COUNT OF CAMPOREAL

MARQUESS OF PRIEGO

DON ANTONIO UBILLA

MONTAZGO

COVADENGA

GUDIEL

A LACKEY

AN USHER

AN OFFICER

A GUARD

A PAGE

QUEEN OF SPAIN

DUCHESS OF ALBUQUERQUE

CASILDA

A DUENNA

Waiting Women, Lords, Privy Councillors, Pages, Duennas, Guards, Mutes, Ushers of the Chamber and the Court

ACT ONE

(Don Sallusto)

The hall of Danae in the Royal Palace in Madrid. The furniture is sumptuous and in the part-Flemish taste in fashion at the time of Philip IV. Left, a large, gilt-latticed window. On either side, on a cant, a low door leading to some interior rooms. Upstage, a large glass partition, also gilt-latticed, in which there is a glass door opening onto a long corridor. This corridor, which runs the entire length of the stage, is hidden by great curtains which fall from the top to the bottom of the glass partition. There is a table, an armchair and writing implements.

DON SALLUSTO enters by the small door stage left, followed by RUY BLAS and GUDIEL, who is carrying a small chest and various other items suggestive of imminent travel. DON SALLUSTO is dressed in black velvet in the court dress of the time of Carlos II. He wears the order of the Golden Fleece around his neck. Over his black tunic, a rich cloak of light velvet embroidered with gold and lined with black satin. He wears a sword with a large basket-hilt and a hat with white feathers. GUDIEL is in black and also wears a sword. RUY BLAS is dressed in livery: brown breeches and jerkin, red- and gold-trimmed overgarment, bare-headed and with no sword. He leaves the door open behind him.

DON SALLUSTO:
    Ruy Blas! The door. And open that window.

    (*RUY BLAS obeys and then, at a sign from DON SALLUSTO, exits by the upstage door. DON SALLUSTO goes to the window.*)

    No-one stirring yet. But soon, when dawn breaks –
    (*He turns abruptly to GUDIEL.*)
    May the flesh rot on their bones, every one!
    Banished, Gudiel, do you hear! My power broken.
    Publicly humiliated, sent packing,
    In one day everything lost! – Not a word
    To anyone till the news is proclaimed –

Yes, and all for some paltry flirtation –
The height of folly at my age, I admit –
But with whom? A mere lady-in-waiting,
A little Miss No-One! Says I seduced her!
A fine mess! And because this whore belongs
To the Queen – came with her from Neubourg –
When she whined about me, dragging her brat
Into the royal apartments, what happened?
I was ordered to marry her! I refused
Of course. And so? I'm sent into exile!
Me, into exile! After twenty years
Of unremitting labour, twenty years
As hated head of the Royal Tribunal,
I at whose mere name all Spain grows pale,
I, proud scion of the House of Bazan,
My authority, my power, all the things
I ever dreamed of, all that I've achieved,
All I possess – offices, functions, honours –
All torn from me in the course of one night
To the common rabble's raucous delight!

GUDIEL:

But, my lord, you said no-one knows it yet.

DON SALLUSTO:

Tomorrow! They will tomorrow! But by then
We will be far away. I don't intend
To 'fall from power', no, I mean to – vanish!
(*Violently unbuttoning his doublet.*)
You always fasten me as one would some priest!
I can barely breathe, this doublet's so tight.
(*He sits.*)
Yes, I intend to burrow, like a mole,
Deep underground, down in the dark, so that
None will suspect beneath their very feet –
(*He stands.*)
Me! Exiled!

GUDIEL: Who passed this sentence, my lord?

DON SALLUSTO:

 The Queen, Gudiel! But I'll have my revenge,
Do you hear me? You, who over the years
Have guided my steps, served my every need,
You know better than any the dark places
My thoughts plumb, just as a good architect
Knows with one practised look the depth of a well
He has sunk. I am leaving here and will first go
To Finlas in Castille, to my estates there,
Where I'll brood awhile – All for some she-flesh!
You're to see to it that all's made ready
For our departure for we must make haste.
But first I will speak with a certain rogue –
One you know well. It may be worth the pains
Since, who knows, he could be put to some use.
I'm still master here till this day's over.
Oh, Gudiel, I'll be revenged! Quite how
Is yet shrouded but I'll see her weep blood!
Go and finish all our preparations.
Quick! And no word. You will be coming too.
(*GUDIEL bows and leaves.*)
Ruy Blas!

(*RUY BLAS appears at the upstage door.*)

RUY BLAS: Your Excellency called?

DON SALLUSTO: Yes.

 I'll not be staying at the palace any more,
So leave the keys and see the shutters are closed.

RUY BLAS: (*Bowing.*)

 Whatever you say, my lord.

DON SALLUSTO: Listen now:

 In two hours' time the Queen will pass along
That corridor on her way back from Mass
To her royal suite. Make sure that you are here
When she passes, Ruy Blas.

RUY BLAS: I will, my lord.

DON SALLUSTO: (*At the window but keeping out of sight.*)
Come here! That man down there in the square – look,
Showing the guards a letter – do you see?
Now he is moving on. Signal to him
Without speaking that he is to come up here
By the back stairs.
(*RUY BLAS does as he is told.*)
Good. But before you leave,
Go and see if the guards there in that room
Are awake yet.

(*RUY BLAS goes to DSR door, half opens it and returns.*)

RUY BLAS: They are still sleeping, my lord.

DON SALLUSTO:
Keep your voice down! I will be needing you
So don't go far. And see we are not disturbed.

(*Enter DON CESAR, a sloppy figure. He and RUY BLAS react in surprise on seeing each other.*)

(*Aside.*) That look between them – do they know each other?

(*RUY BLAS exits.*)

So there you are, you old brigand!

DON CESAR: Yes, cousin,
Here I am indeed.

DON SALLUSTO: What a pleasure to see
An old ragamuffin such as yourself!

DON CESAR: (*Bowing.*)
You are too kind.

DON SALLUSTO: (*Mock chiding.*) But I have been hearing
Tales about you.

DON CESAR: I trust they are to your liking?

DON SALLUSTO:
Oh, most praiseworthy! Why, the other night
Don Carlos de Mira was foully robbed
Of his fine sword with its engraved scabbard
And buff leather belt. This on Good Friday
Of all days! Though, as knight of the Order
Of St James, he was kindly spared his cloak.

DON CESAR:
Good Lord! And why did they do that?

DON SALLUSTO: The sign
Of the Order was embroidered on the hem?
So, and what do you say to this street violence?

DON CESAR:
Hell and damnation, but I say we're living
In a dreadful age! What in Heaven's name
Is to become of us all if thieves now grovel
Before St James and take his part... ?

DON SALLUSTO: You were
Of their number?

DON CESAR: Well, if pressed, yes, I was.
But I laid not one finger on the said
Gentleman – I simply offered advice.

DON SALLUSTO:
There's more. Last night was moonless: a motley crew
Of half-dressed vagabonds, vomiting forth
From some hell-hole on the Plaza Major,
Ran amok and attacked the night guard – you
Were of their number.

DON CESAR: Cousin, to lock horns
With those who keep the peace I've ever held
Beneath contempt. It is true, I was there
But not drawn. During all the cut and thrust
I walked about under the arcade, wrestling
Only with my Muse – composing verses.
But heads rolled, I can tell you!

DON SALLUSTO: And there's more.

DON CESAR:
Let's hear it, then.

DON SALLUSTO: In France you are accused,
Along with a band of lawless companions,
Of having, amongst other felonies,
Broken open the cash box of the tax
Collectors and –

171

DON CESAR: That I will not deny.
  The French are our enemies.

DON SALLUSTO: Then in Flanders
  A certain Father Paul Barthelemy,
  Returning to his noble Chapter in Mons
  With a full purse from the sale of produce
  Grown on their vineyard, was seized and relieved
  Of this same purse – property of the Church!

DON CESAR:
  In Flanders, you say? Yes, that could well be:
  I do travel widely. Is that all now?

DON SALLUSTO:
  Don Cesar, when I think of you I blush
  So deeply that I break out in a sweat –

DON CESAR:
  Blush away, dear fellow!

DON SALLUSTO: Our family –

DON CESAR: (*Lowering his voice.*)
  Please, no talk of family! My real name's
  Known only to you and so I'd have it stay.

DON SALLUSTO:
  Well, well. Coming out of church the other day
  A Marchioness turned to me and enquired:
  'Who is that brigand yonder, nose in the air,
  Gazing about him and strutting around
  One hip to the fore? Though more down-at-heel
  Than your Job ever was, yet he appears
  Haughtier than a Turk – his wretchedness
  Hidden beneath a puffed-up veil of pride.
  See how, below a tattered sleeve, his hand
  Now kneads the heavy pommel of his sword
  Whose tip in turn knocks and chafes at his heels.
  Thus he promenades with lordly aplomb,
  Despite a cloak more like a beggar's rags
  And hose that hang like dripping candle-wax.'

DON CESAR: (*Glancing at his own person.*)
And so you said: 'It's my friend, Zafari!'

DON SALLUSTO:
No, sir, I blushed.

DON CESAR: The lady was amused
At least – delighting ladies delights me.

DON SALLUSTO:
Your sole companions are rogues and ruffians!

DON CESAR:
Scholars each one! Students of religion
And as gentle as lambs.

DON SALLUSTO: Aside from these
It's sluts and whores who hang about your neck.

DON CESAR:
Juliets! Rosalinds! Sweet Esmeraldas!
With which I hear you are plentifully supplied.
Are you as well served? Ah, those dark beauties
With their roguish eyes! At night I read them
The sonnets I've penned them during the day...

DON SALLUSTO:
And, to cap it all, that Galician thief,
Matalobos, who, evading all capture,
Still strikes terror in the heart of Madrid –
This villain, too, you count among your friends!

DON CESAR:
Be reasonable now – if it weren't for him
I'd have to parade in the town stark naked:
Seeing me half-dressed in the streets last winter
Moved him so, that – well, the Count of Alba,
That amber-perfumed fop, recently lost
His fine, silken doublet and so –

DON SALLUSTO: Yes? So?

DON CESAR:
Well, now it's mine, thanks to Matalobos.

DON SALLUSTO:
The Count's – ? Aren't you ashamed?

DON CESAR: Ashamed? Never!
What, a fine doublet, beautifully embroidered,
With lace trim, warm in winter, smart in summer – ?
Look, it's hardly worn!
(*He partially opens his cloak to reveal a superb doublet of pink satin embroidered in gold.*)
                              The pockets were stuffed
With billets doux. Often, when short of funds
And hungry thus for food as well as love,
I swear I can smell cooking wafting from
These pages, gushing out hotly as from
A kitchen vent! – and so I sit and read them
Closely, thus. And by gulling in this way
Both stomach and heart, my nose feasts my head
On the double joys of both board and bed!

DON SALLUSTO:
Don Cesar –

DON CESAR: Cousin, please, cease your complaints.
I am, it's true, a lord and near to you
In blood: Don Cesar, Count of Garofa;
But though by my birth fate raised me up high,
She withheld the wit that might have kept me there:
I was rich, had palaces and estates
And so could entertain ladies galore
But damn me if I was not yet come of age
When riotous living had devoured the lot!
All that remained to me was a hungry pack
Of baying creditors closing in for the kill.
So I simply disappeared and took the name
'Zafari', which is what I am today,
Drinking companion and night carouser,
Unrecognizable to all but you.
Everyone else thinks Don Cesar has gone
To the New World – that is, to the devil –
And is, in short, dead. Long may they think so!
From you I receive not one single sou
And so I do without. For nine years now
I've slept in front of the ancient palace

Of the Counts of Tera, beneath my head
A stone pillow, above the blanketing sky.
And I am happy thus – it's a good life,
I can tell you. Nearby there's a fountain
Where, after freshening up, I will stroll
About and hold my head up with the rest.
My former residence, that great tombstone
That hides the corpse of all my worldly wealth,
Is now owned by the Papal Nuncio,
One Espinola. Over the portico
Workmen are carving a Bacchus and so,
Whenever I'm passing, I drop them the odd
Hint or two…but for the present, cousin,
You couldn't see your way to lending me
Ten crowns, could you?

DON SALLUSTO: Listen –

DON CESAR: (*Folding his arms.*)   I'm listening.

DON SALLUSTO:

I sent for you to offer you my help:
I have no children, I am rich and also
Your elder by some years, so it pains me,
Cesar, to see you sliding every day
Deeper into the abyss – it is my intent
To pull you out of it altogether.
However much you may swagger about,
You are, to speak truth, in a sorry state.
I will settle all your debts, return you
Your palace, re-establish you at Court
And change you back to the gallant you were –
Let Zafari die and Cesar be reborn!
You are, without reserve, to make free use
Of all my fortune, to plunge your hands in
Up to the elbows with no thought for the morrow!
To kith and kin we should open – dear Cesar –
The strings of our purse with those of our heart.
(*DON CESAR's face has been a study of growing astonishment
and radiant delight. He now bursts out:*)

175

DON CESAR:
>Why, you've a dry wit! And always have had.
>A very devil. But do go on!

DON SALLUSTO: One
>Condition alone I make, dear Cesar –
>I'll tell you straight but here, first take this purse.

DON CESAR: (*Weighing the purse which is full of gold.*)
>This is wonderful indeed.

DON SALLUSTO: A further
>Five hundred ducats I will add to this
>As an allowance –

DON CESAR: (*Dumbfounded.*) Marquess!

DON SALLUSTO: – from today.

DON CESAR:
>By Heaven, I'm yours, to do with as you please!
>As for this condition, let's hear it, but
>By my honour as a true, fighting man,
>I am your slave, ready to do your will,
>Were it to cross swords with Satan in Hell!

DON SALLUSTO:
>For reasons I'll give I can't accept your sword.

DON CESAR:
>Then what? There's damn all else I have to offer.

DON SALLUSTO: (*Approaching him with lowered voice.*)
>You are on good terms with all the scoundrels
>In Madrid, are you not?

DON CESAR: You flatter me.

DON SALLUSTO:
>You always have a pack of curs in tow
>And could, therefore, should the need arise,
>Start a riot, say? Yes, I'm sure you could.
>Something of that sort could prove quite useful.

DON CESAR: (*Bursting out with laughter.*)
>Is it some opera you have in mind?
>And how can my talents be of service?
>Am I to write the lyrics or the music?

Either way I'm your man and no mistake:
Past master at keeping neighbours awake.

DON SALLUSTO: (*Gravely.*)

My suit's to Don Cesar, not Zafari.
(*He lowers his voice yet further.*)
Listen. I need a man of steel to lurk
In the shadows and help me bring about
A deed of great note. I am not disposed
To base actions but this affair is such
The daintiest stomach would cast aside
All scruples to execute my purpose.
Your former fortune I vow to restore
If you agree to help me lay a snare
Like men at night who with nets of fine mesh
Hidden beneath the lure of glinting glass
Trap themselves birds – or girls, as well they might.
Some such snare, something cunning and cruel –
And you're not known to be tender-hearted –
I must devise to obtain my revenge.

DON CESAR:

You seek revenge?

DON SALLUSTO: Yes.

DON CESAR: On whom?

DON SALLUSTO: A woman.

DON CESAR: (*He straightens up again and looks proudly at*
    DON SALLUSTO.)

A woman? Then I'll not hear one word more!
You astound me, cousin – what, any man
Worthy of a sword and yet who basely
And by subtle means seeks to take revenge
On a woman and who thus, although born
A gentleman, deserves the title of slave,
Such a man, be he Castillian lord
Whom fanfares of brass herald the approach,
Whose marks and whose insignia of rank
Festoon him from toe to crown in pure gold,
Be he a Marquess, Viscount, one who can trace

177

A noble line that reaches back to the Ark,
Such a man I prize of no greater worth
Than a sly, devious and cowardly dog,
One it would gladden me hugely to see
Dangling dead from the nearest gallows tree!

DON SALLUSTO:
Cesar!

DON CESAR: I said not a word! It's quite outrageous.
Keep your secret –
(*Throwing purse down at his feet.*)
                   – yes, and your money, too!
Stealing, now, killing, ransacking, looting,
These I understand; taking a castle
In a night assault, with halberd in hand
And a hundred rogues roaring at your side;
Cutting the throats of flunkeys and jailers;
Hacking and howling like the brigands we are;
Giving rough justice, an eye for an eye –
All this I can accept – men against men;
But to seek in cold blood to destroy a woman,
Dig pitfalls beneath her feet, exploiting,
Say, her lack of discretion to snare her
Thus horribly in lime, the poor creature;
To be at such a price a rich lord again –
And here I call on God to be my witness –
To suffer such dishonour, sink so low,
Be so despicable, wretched and base,
Far rather set me naked in the stocks
Where my bones can be gnawed by mangy dogs!

DON SALLUSTO:
My dear cousin – !

DON CESAR: And the loss of your offer
I'll regret not one jot, just so long as
Fountains hold water and meadows fresh air,
In Madrid there's a thief who'll keep me warm,
In my soul there's disdain for vanished wealth,
And before your palace there are large gates

Where in the noonday heat I can lay me down,
My head in the shade, my feet in the sun,
And sleep, letting whatever comes come.

DON SALLUSTO:
One moment –

DON CESAR: This interview is at an end.
If now you intend to put me behind bars,
Then do so, please; let's get it over with.

DON SALLUSTO:
Well, well, Cesar, and there was I thinking
You were past cure and beyond redemption.
Well done! Magnificent! You stood the test –
Give me your hand.

DON CESAR: Why?

DON SALLUSTO: It was all in jest.
Simply a trial. Nothing more.

DON CESAR: You mean
That woman, your scheming, your lust for revenge
Was something I heard in some waking dream?

DON SALLUSTO:
A bait. Pure fantasy! Painted in air.

DON CESAR:
Well, I'm relieved to hear it, I must confess!
And your offer to settle all my debts,
The five hundred ducats, did I dream that, too?

DON SALLUSTO:
No, that I meant. I'll fetch them for you now.
(*He goes to the upstage door and signals RUY BLAS to enter.*)

DON CESAR: (*Aside and with a wary look at the other.*)
A Judas face! Even his features conflict:
The 'No' of his lips his eyes contradict.

DON SALLUSTO: (*To RUY BLAS.*)
Wait in here, Ruy Blas.
(*Turning back to DON CESAR.*)
                        I'll be with you straight.

(*DON SALLUSTO leaves by the small door stage left. As
soon as he is gone, DON CESAR and RUY BLAS turn to
face each other.*)

DON CESAR:

By heaven, I was right: it *is* you, Ruy Blas!

RUY BLAS:

Zafari! It's you! But what brings you here?

DON CESAR:

Just – visiting. But I'm on my way now.
Like the birds I need room to spread my wings.
And yourself? This livery you're wearing –
(*Lowering his voice.*)
Are you in disguise?

RUY BLAS: (*Bitterly.*)   No. This is what I am.
Anything but this would be a disguise.

DON CESAR:

What do you mean?

RUY BLAS: Come, let me embrace you!
Oh, Zafari, those times we spent together –
The laughter, the sorrow – our only roof
The sky above! By day racked with hunger,
By night with cold, yet could I call myself
Free then, and a man. How long ago now!
Looking so alike we were thought brothers –
And so we were: both sons of the people!
All day, from first light, we'd sing our hearts out
And at night bed down in that hostelry
Where Heaven's myriad eyes watched over us;
And, until that day when our roads parted,
Everything we had we shared between us.
But here you are again after four years
Quite unchanged: as cheerful as ever, as
Free as the wind, the same old Zafari:
Rich in having and desiring nothing.
And here I am – but what a change indeed!
I was an orphan whom charity gave

A schooling which bred in me naught but pride,
Nurtured not diligence but a thousand dreams –
But this you know. Oh, what a pair we made:
I, defying Heaven with wild verses
Of hope and you, laughing them all to scorn!
Such dreams I had then – all forgotten now –
That made labour seem vain, for I was bound
For some invisible goal, and, deeming
All things possible, trusted wholly in
Whatever destiny might bring. I'd spend
Days on end deep in thought, lounging before
Some fine palace fairly bulging with wealth,
Watching great ladies coming in and out.
On such a day it was that, nearly dead
With hunger, a jewelled hand reached out with bread:
I took it, ate, and stilled my belly's pangs
But damned my soul to craven indolence.
Oh, when I was twenty and dreamt of greatness,
I would walk around barefoot, lost in thought,
Constructing in my head such grand projects,
So many, piled up, they'd have pierced the clouds!
I bewailed the misfortunes of Spain, believed
That the world lacked but for one thing: myself!
And what became of such a grand idea?
The world lacked but for the lackey you see here!

DON CESAR:
When need thrusts us down through hunger's low door
It is the greatest who must bend the most.
But life ebbs and flows: you must not lose hope.

RUY BLAS: (*Shaking his head.*)
The man I serve is the Marquess of Finlas.

DON CESAR:
Yes, I know him. Do you live in this palace?

RUY BLAS:
No. Until this morning – until just now –
I had never crossed its threshold before.

181

DON CESAR:

> Yes? But surely your master's position
> Requires he live at the centre of power?

RUY BLAS:

> Of course, and he does, but not far from here
> He has secret lodgings to which he repairs
> Only at half-light, a modest dwelling
> And all I have known till today. Sometimes
> The Marquess returns there at night, by a door
> To which only he has the key, with a troop
> Of hooded men who speak all in whispers.
> What then goes on once the doors are tight shut
> No-one can say for my sole companions
> Are two black mutes who think I'm their master
> And are even ignorant as to my name.

DON CESAR:

> That must be where, as head of the Tribunal,
> He confers with his spies and spins his webs –
> In darkness he lives but has eyes everywhere.

RUY BLAS:

> Yesterday he told me to be here at dawn,
> To use the main gate, and when I arrived
> He made me put on these clothes, this hated
> Livery that I wear for the first time.

DON CESAR: (*Pressing his hand.*)

> You must not despair.

RUY BLAS: No? But there's more:

> The blackest part of my tale's yet to come.
> To live in a slave's garb, soiled, dishonoured,
> To have lost all happiness, all self-respect,
> This is a trifle, for the shame I might feel
> Wearing this livery is as nothing
> To the horror of that which rages within:
> There lives a monster with teeth of fire
> Whose burning coils are twined about my heart –
> A swirl of water is all that betrays
> The clash of Titans below.

DON CESAR: What do you mean?

RUY BLAS:

    Give your fantasy wings and let her soar
    High above what's commonplace, what's mundane,
    To seek out strange worlds never glimpsed before
    Where disasters like mine are everyday.
    No, you could never divine my secret,
    Look down rather into that dark abyss
    Where fate hurls wretches who dare to dream
    And there see a lackey – in love with a Queen!

DON CESAR:

    God in Heaven!

RUY BLAS: Beneath a canopy
    Embellished with the globe imperial,
    In Aranjuez or in the Escurial,
    Or sometimes here in this palace, there sits
    A man the likes of us will never see.
    His name, when uttered, awakens terror,
    While before him all are equal, as with God.
    Those who may look on him serve him trembling
    On their knees; to stand in his presence, head
    Covered, is an honour of the highest order –
    One nod of his could make both ours roll.
    His every whim an event of note,
    He lives set apart and in proud splendour,
    Encompassed on all sides by a majesty
    So awesome, so sacred and so immense
    It casts its shadow over half the known world.
    And this man who makes the sun's glory dim
    I, a lackey, I, am jealous of him.

DON CESAR:

    Jealous of the King?

RUY BLAS: Yes. That's how things stand.
    Jealous – because I'm in love with his wife.

DON CESAR:

    Oh, you unhappy fellow!

RUY BLAS: Every day
   Like one possessed, I wait to see her pass.
   And this sad lady is chained to a life
   Of endless misery. I think of her
   Each night, living there at Court in the midst
   Of the hatred and lies, married to a King
   Who spends his time hunting from dawn to dusk –
   A half-wit, a dolt, senile at thirty!
   A freak, unfit to live, let alone to reign!
   His blood is corrupt – they say his father
   Couldn't hold a paper, his hands shook so.
   And she – so beautiful, so young – to have
   Given herself to this Carlos the Second!
   How wretched she must feel! Every evening
   She visits the Sisters of the Rosary
   In Ortaleza street – do you know it?
   How things grew to such a pitch of madness
   I cannot say, but there's a flower she loves –
   Listen to this and then you'll understand –
   A small, blue flower which thrives in her homeland
   So every day I ride to Carabanchel –
   A good league from here and the only place
   I have found it growing – to pick her some.
   I make a bouquet of the prettiest blooms;
   Then, at midnight – sheer madness you will say –
   I slip like a thief into the Royal park
   And place the flowers on her favourite bench –
   Today I even dared to include a letter.
   It's true, brother! Come, show some sympathy:
   To reach that bench at night I have to climb
   The park walls which, like jawbones of stone,
   Sprout iron fangs! I tell you, one fine day
   I'll get sliced up fit for a butcher's slab!
   But the flowers and letter I left last night,
   I must know if she's found them already...
   Do you see now the enormity of my plight?

DON CESAR:

    Damn me but you're treading on dangerous ground:
    The Count of Onato also loves her,
    Jealously watches her with a jailer's eye –
    One night, before your bouquet's even begun
    To wilt, you'll find it skewered to your heart,
    Both impaled on the pike-staff of some guard
    After advancement. But in love with the Queen?
    What devil prompted this? And tell me, when – ?

RUY BLAS: (*With passion and then turning to the window.*)

    How should I know! But I would sell my soul
    To that same devil to be one of those
    Nobles swaggering in there down below
    In all their feathers – mockeries of men!
    Yes, I would damn myself eternally
    To be rid of these chains, able to approach
    The Queen like them, honourably attired.
    But to have to be in her presence like this?
    In front of them? It's more than I can stand!
    Harnessed and yoked in the garb of a slave,
    And for her to think me one – God forbid!
    (*Turning back to DON CESAR.*)
    But you asked how it was I came to love her,
    When it began: one day, it was – but what's
    The use? Questions, questions! Always you would
    Torture me with endless questions, like where
    And how, when and why – it's enough you know
    I love and adore her – worship her – oh! –

DON CESAR:

    Calm yourself, my friend.

RUY BLAS: (*Falling pale and exhausted into an armchair.*)
                    I'm sorry, Zafari,
    But I'm on the rack! You were best advised
    To keep a safe distance, leave such a fool
    To the pain of feeling in his heart a king
    But dressed a slave, a cipher, a mere thing!

DON CESAR: (*Placing a hand on his shoulder.*)
I leave you? I who have never suffered
Since I have never really loved – a sad bell
Without the clapper that would make it ring.
A tramp, who must beg for love in strange places
And who now and then is thrown a chance crumb,
Whose heart has guttered, its flame a curl of smoke,
Or like last month's playbill, peeling and torn –
So while I pity you in your agony
I envy its cause – no such love for me!

(*A moment of silence. They remain grasping each other by the hand and looking at each other with an expression of trusting friendship. DON SALLUSTO meanwhile has entered and been watching the two very attentively – they do not see him. In one hand he carries a hat and sword which he places on an armchair, and in the other a purse of money which he places on the table.*)

DON SALLUSTO: (*To DON CESAR.*)
Here is the money.

(*At the sound of DON SALLUSTO's voice, RUY BLAS and DON CESAR start abruptly, the former quickly resuming a respectful attitude with eyes lowered.*)

DON CESAR: (*Aside and scowling at DON SALLUSTO.*)
                    I'd wager all he's brought
That sly fellow was listening at the door.
But to hell! What does it matter if he was!
(*Aloud and taking the purse.*)
Thank you, Don Sallusto!

(*DON CESAR opens the purse, spreads out the contents on the table, handling the coins with obvious delight and arranging them into two heaps on the velvet cloth. While he is counting them out, DON SALLUSTO goes upstage, watching carefully lest he should attract the attention of DON CESAR. He opens the small, right-hand door. At a sign from him, three guards emerge, dressed in black and with swords. In secretive fashion DON SALLUSTO points out DON CESAR to them.*)

RUY BLAS, *meanwhile, is standing by the table as still as stone, without seeing or hearing anything.*)

DON SALLUSTO: (*Low, to the guards.*) The one counting
The coins, him you're to follow when he leaves.
Then, unobserved, seize him – no violence, mind –
And take him post-haste to the port of Denia.
(*Handing them a sealed paper.*)
Here is the order written in my hand.
His mind's a nest of lies – pay them no heed.
Once at sea, sell him to the Arab traders –
A thousand piastres wait your safe return.

(*The men bow and leave.*)

DON CESAR: (*Concluding the sorting of his ducats.*)
Nothing entertains or gives more delight
Than building two gold towers of equal height!
(*To RUY BLAS.*)
Here you are, brother: this is your share.

RUY BLAS: What?

DON CESAR:
Like in the old days – come, no need to be shy!

DON SALLUSTO: (*Aside, looking at one, then the other.*)
In the devil's name –

RUY BLAS: (*Shaking his head.*) Those times are over.
Now I have left me but one single care,
My life one aim, my soul one constant prayer.

DON CESAR:
Very well – if you must make dreams your goal –
But whether you're the madman and I the sage,
That God alone can say.

(*He gathers up the money and puts it back into the purse which he then pockets.*)

DON SALLUSTO: (*From upstage and watching them continuously; aside:*)   – in both manner
And appearance they could be taken for twins –

DON CESAR: (*To RUY BLAS.*)
Farewell.

RUY BLAS: Give me your hand.

(*DON CESAR does so and then leaves, oblivious of DON SALLUSTO's presence.*)

DON SALLUSTO: Ruy Blas!

RUY BLAS: (*Turning swiftly.*)   My lord?

DON SALLUSTO:

How light was it today when you first arrived?

RUY BLAS:

It was pitch black, my lord. I showed the guard
The pass you gave me and came straight up.

DON SALLUSTO:

Were you wearing a cloak?

RUY BLAS: I was, my lord.

DON SALLUSTO:

So no-one here has seen you dressed like this?

RUY BLAS:

Save your last visitor, no-one in Madrid.

DON SALLUSTO:

Excellent. Good.
(*Indicating the door by which DON CESAR left.*)
                        Close that door. Then remove
Your livery.
(*RUY BLAS obeys, throwing the livery into the armchair.*)
                  You've a fine hand, I think –
(*Signalling him to sit at the writing table.*)
Today you will serve me as secretary.
First, a love letter – you see, there's nothing
I conceal from you – to my Queen of Love,
Dona Praxedis – a fiend who can open
The gates to paradise. So, I'll dictate:
'I stand in great peril. Only my Queen
Can shield me from the deadly lightning bolt.
Let her come to my house tonight, else I am lost.
My life, my head, my heart, lie at her feet
On which I plant this kiss, pure and discreet.'
(*Laughing.*)

'Stand in great peril'! Quite good, don't you think?
That should bring her running. Take it from me,
Women perform best for the men who use them worst –
I know. Add: 'To avoid being recognised,
Enter the house by the last door you'll come to.
Someone of the highest trust will be there
To let you in.' Perfect, by my life! Now, sign.

RUY BLAS:
Your name, my lord?

DON SALLUSTO: No, no. Sign it 'Cesar'.
My 'nom de guerre'!

RUY BLAS: (*After signing.*) But she won't know the hand.

DON SALLUSTO: She will the seal. I often correspond
With her in this fashion. Now, Ruy Blas,
I am leaving tonight. But you will remain.
I have plans for you born of a good will:
You are to undergo a change in your condition
But continue to obey me in all things.
Since I have found you dependable and true –

RUY BLAS: (*Standing and bowing.*)
My lord.

DON SALLUSTO: – so would I now broaden for you
The horizons of your life.

RUY BLAS: (*Indicating the letter he has written.*)
                        What address
Should I write, my lord?

DON SALLUSTO: I will see to that.
(*Approaching RUY BLAS with knowing emphasis.*)
I desire your welfare.
(*He signals RUY BLAS to be seated once more.*)
                        Now write down this:
'I, Ruy Blas, lackey to his lordship
The Marquess of Finlas, vow at all times
And in all places both private and public
To serve the said lord in all dutifulness
As a true retainer of his noble house.'

(*RUY BLAS obeys.*)
Sign it with your own name. And then the date.
Good. Now give it to me.
(*He folds both letter and paper, putting them away in a case.*)

I see a sword
Has been brought in – over there on the chair –
(*Fetching it.*)
The strap is of silk, dyed and embroidered
In the very latest fashion. There, feel it!
(*Inviting him to test the smoothness of the fabric, he passes him the weapon.*)
So what do you think of this foil, Ruy Blas?
The hilt is the work of the master craftsman,
Gil, who in the pommel of his swords secretes
A box for sweetmeats as bait for pretty girls.
Come! Put it on now –
(*Putting the strap over RUY BLAS's head.*)

I would like to see
What it looks like on you. But I do declare
You look the perfect gentleman! My word,
Every inch a lord! (*He stops to listen.*)

Yes, they are coming.
The Queen will soon be passing this way. Ah!
The Marquess of Basto!

(*The door opens at the end of the corridor. DON SALLUSTO takes off his cloak and swiftly throws it over RUY BLAS's shoulders at the moment when the MARQUESS OF BASTO appears, whom he now approaches, pulling the bewildered RUY BLAS after him.*)

Do me the honour,
My lord Marquess, and kindly allow me
To present to you my cousin, Don Cesar,
Count of Garofa, near Velalcazar.

RUY BLAS: (*Aside.*)
Good God!

DON SALLUSTO: (*Low to RUY BLAS.*)
          Quiet now!

MARQUESS OF BASTO: (*To RUY BLAS.*)
                Delighted, I'm sure, sir –
(*He takes the hand RUY BLAS awkwardly offers him.*)

DON SALLUSTO: (*Low to RUY BLAS.*)
Go with the tide, man! Greet him properly!
(*RUY BLAS greets the MARQUESS OF BASTO.*)

MARQUESS OF BASTO:
I simply adored your dear late mother!
(*Low to DON SALLUSTO.*)
He's greatly changed! I scarce would have known him.

DON SALLUSTO: (*Low to MARQUESS OF BASTO.*)
He's been away ten years.

MARQUESS OF BASTO: (*Low to DON SALLUSTO.*)
                Away with you!

DON SALLUSTO: (*Slapping RUY BLAS on the shoulder.*)
But now, as you can see, he has returned!
Do you remember, Marquess, the lad he was?
Such a prodigal, he scattered money
Like a dog shakes water out of his coat!
Every evening revelling and feasting
Down by Apollo's Pool, a huge orchestra
Out on the lake playing with such gusto
The dead were like to have danced! Then the endless
Galas, masques, concerts – oh and the japes!
And spectacles too that left all Madrid
Gasping for breath! And then, after three years,
Ruined! Ah, yes, a true society lion.
But back now, laden – not, I might add, with iron!

RUY BLAS: (*In confusion.*)
My lord –

DON SALLUSTO: (*Gaily.*) Cousin! Call me cousin! That's what
We are, after all. We Bazans have big hearts.
Iniguez d'Iviza was our ancestor
And his grandson was Pedro de Bazan,

191

Whose wife was Marianne de Gor. By her
He had a son, Jean, later admiral
Under King Philip. This Jean had two sons:
These were they who grafted two different
Coats-of-arms onto our family tree.
I, the Marquess of Finlas, and you, the Count
Of Garofa, are yet of equal rank
On the maternal side, for I belong
To the Portuguese branch, you to Aragon,
A branch, please note, that's not one whit lower –
I the ripe fruit, you the budding flower!

RUY BLAS: (*Aside.*)
Where is he dragging me? My name is Ruy Blas –

(*While DON SALLUSTO has been speaking, the
MARQUESS OF SANTA CRUZ, DON ALVAR DE BAZAN
Y BENAVIDES, has approached, an old man with white
moustache and a large wig.*)

SANTA CRUZ: (*To DON SALLUSTO.*)
Well said! But a cousin of yours is mine, too.

DON SALLUSTO:
That's true, Marquess. We spring from the same trunk.
The Marquess of Santa Cruz –
(*Presenting him to RUY BLAS.*) – Don Cesar!

SANTA CRUZ:
Surely not the one assumed to be dead?

DON SALLUSTO:
The very same.

SANTA CRUZ: Then he has returned from the…?

DON SALLUSTO:
New World.

SANTA CRUZ: (*Examining RUY BLAS.*)
Indeed?

DON SALLUSTO: Do you recognise him?

SANTA CRUZ:
Good heavens! I was present at his birth.

DON SALLUSTO: (*Aside to RUY BLAS.*)
    As blind as a worm – and a liar to boot:
    He'd swear he knew you to prove his sight good.

SANTA CRUZ: (*Extending a hand to RUY BLAS.*)
    My hand, cousin.

RUY BLAS: (*Taking his hand and bowing.*)
                    My lord –

SANTA CRUZ:
    (*Aside to DON SALLUSTO indicating RUY BLAS.*)
                            Peerless, cousin!
    Simply peerless!
    (*To RUY BLAS.*) Charmed to see you again!

DON SALLUSTO: (*Taking SANTA CRUZ aside.*)
    I intend, cousin, to settle all his debts.
    Now you would be well placed to assist him, too,
    If some post became vacant, say, attending
    On the King – or even the Queen – here at Court.

SANTA CRUZ:
    A charming young man! Yes, I'll give it some thought –
    After all, he *is* family.

DON SALLUSTO: Your voice
    In the Council of Castille carries weight –
    Well, I recommend him to you, cousin.
    (*Turns and presents RUY BLAS to others and then to the
    COUNT OF ALBA, who is magnificently accoutred.*)
    My cousin, Don Cesar, Count of Garofa,
    Near Velalcazar.
    (*The lords all gravely exchange bows with the speechless RUY
    BLAS. DON SALLUSTO addresses the COUNT OF
    RIBAGORZA:*)
                    You missed the ballet
    Yesterday, I hear. Atalanta? Ah,
    Lindamire – she danced like a dream!
    (*He turns to admire the COUNT OF ALBA's doublet.*)
                            Oh, my
    Dear Count of Alba! That really is fine!

COUNT ALBA:

Yes, but I had one much finer than this –
In pink satin it was, with gold braiding –
But that Matalobos stole it from me.

USHER: (*From upstage.*)

Her Royal Majesty the Queen approaches!
To your stations, gentlemen, if you please!

(*The great curtains hitherto drawn across the windowed section of the corridor now open. The nobles arrange themselves near the door. The guards form a line. RUY BLAS, in a state of extreme agitation, comes downstage as if in search of an escape. DON SALLUSTO follows him.*)

DON SALLUSTO:

Just when a new world opens wide its arms
Do you now shrink away and seek to hide?
Listen, Ruy Blas! I am leaving Madrid.
I give you my house near the bridge where you lodge –
The mutes as well – everything, save only
The secret keys, is yours. In due course
You will receive fresh orders from me.
Do my bidding and I will make your fortune.
Climb, man, climb and cast aside all fear:
See, the mountains beckon, your hour draws near!
Though the Court's wreathed in mist, to gain your prize
You may walk blindfold, yet see – with my eyes!

(*More guards appear upstage.*)

USHER: (*In a loud voice.*)

Her Royal Majesty, the Queen of Spain!

RUY BLAS: (*Aside.*)

The Queen!

(*The QUEEN, dressed magnificently, appears surrounded by ladies and pages under a canopy of scarlet velvet carried by four bare-headed gentlemen of the Chamber. Aghast, RUY BLAS watches as if paralysed by this dazzling vision. All the noblemen cover their heads. DON SALLUSTO moves swiftly to the chair, recovers the hat, brings it to RUY BLAS and places it on his head.*)

DON SALLUSTO: (*To RUY BLAS.*)

        Here! You're a lord! Not some scatterbrain!

RUY BLAS: (*In a daze.*)

  And my orders, sir? – What am I to do?

DON SALLUSTO: (*Pointing to the QUEEN who is progressing slowly along the corridor.*)

  Woo that woman! Make her fall in love with you!

End of Act One

ACT TWO

(The Queen of Spain)

A room adjoining the Queen's bedchamber. Left, a small door leading to the same; right, in a cant, another door leading to the outer rooms; upstage, large, open windows.

A beautiful summer afternoon – 29th June. A large table. Armchairs. On the wall, the richly-inlaid head of a saint, bearing the legend 'Santa Maria Esclava'; on the opposite side, a Madonna in front of which a gold lamp is burning; near the Madonna hangs a full-length portrait of Carlos II.

When the curtain rises, the QUEEN, dona Maria of Neubourg, is seated in one corner next to one of her women, CASILDA, a pretty young girl. The Queen is in a white dress made of cloth of silver. She is engaged in some embroidery which she interrupts every so often in order to converse. Seated on a high-backed chair in the opposite corner is dona Juana de la Cueva, DUCHESS OF ALBUQUERQUE, the First Lady of the Queen's Bedchamber (Camerara Mayor); she is an old woman, dressed in black and has some tapestry work on her lap. Near the DUCHESS and seated at a table are several other duennas busy with other women's work. Upstage stands DON GURITAN, Count of Onato and Chief Steward, a tall and gaunt man of about fifty-five with a grey moustache; he has the bearing of an old soldier, despite being dressed with exaggerated elegance and having ribbons reaching down to his shoes.

QUEEN:
　Gone – at last! Yet, though I should feel relieved,
　His hatred haunts me still, gnaws at my heart.

CASILDA:
　I thought you had banished the Marquess, ma'am.

QUEEN:
　Such hatred!

CASILDA:　　Didn't you, your Majesty?

QUEEN:

> Yes, Casilda, he is banished yet still here:
> Here in spirit – like an angel of death.
> The day before he was to take his leave
> He came to the ritual kissing of hands;
> In line all the grandees approached the throne;
> In sombre mood I offered them my hand
> While gazing abstractedly through the gloom
> At a huge battle-scene painted on the wall –
> Suddenly, lowering my eyes once more,
> There was this brute bearing down on me!
> The sight of him excluded all sights else:
> I watched as he advanced, slow and grim,
> Toying with the dagger slung at his side
> Whose blade appeared fitfully, flashing threats;
> His eyes were burning, almost blinding mine,
> When all at once, writhing, squirming, down he dips
> And fastens on my hand his cold, snake lips.

CASILDA: (*Laughing.*)

> He was paying you homage! Like we all do.

QUEEN: *His* mouth felt different. Not like the others.

> And though I have not seen him again since then
> I can't stop thinking of him – though Heaven knows
> I have troubles enough – yet I tell myself
> Something demonic dwells within that man:
> His look soils me, strips me of all my worth.
> At night I dream I'm walking down a road
> When this fiend leaps out and seizes my hand –
> His eyes glow with hate, he lowers his head
> And I feel this cold kiss enter my veins
> Like black venom, spreading wave after wave
> Till it reaches my heart, turns it to ice! –
> Well, Casilda?

CASILDA:　　　　A dream, an empty dream!

QUEEN:

> It's true I have cares of greater substance –
> (*Aside.*)
> Torments rather that must remain hidden.

(To CASILDA.)
Tell me, Casilda, those timid beggars...

CASILDA: *(Rising and going to window.)*
Yes, ma'am. They're still waiting down in the square.

QUEEN:
Here, throw them my purse.
(CASILDA takes the purse and goes to throw it out.)

CASILDA: Your Majesty gives
Alms so generously, will she not throw
The Count of Onato a single crumb? Please?
*(Indicating DON GURITAN who stands silently upstage
gazing at the QUEEN with an expression of dumb adoration.)*
One word? An old knight beneath whose chain mail
A broken heart burrows like a purblind mole.

QUEEN:
He's really most vexing.

CASILDA: True. But speak to him.

QUEEN: *(Turning to the COUNT.)*
Good day, Count.

*(DON GURITAN approaches the QUEEN bowing three
times. Sighing, he kisses her hand which she absently extends
to him with an air of indifference. Then he returns to his
place next to the chair of the Camerara Mayor, the
DUCHESS.)*

DON GURITAN: *(Low to CASILDA as he retires.)*
                Entrancing – the Queen today!

CASILDA: *(Watching him cross to his place.)*
The poor old heron! He stands all day long
By the tempting water's edge and spears perhaps
A cold and scaly 'greeting' once a week?
Then blissfully stalks off, this scrap in his beak.

QUEEN: *(With a sad smile.)*
Casilda!

CASILDA: To gaze at you is his sole joy!
(Seeing a box on a low, round table.)
Oh, what a splendid box!

QUEEN: Yes – here's the key.

CASILDA: Made of aloes. Mmm – divine!

QUEEN: (*Offering her the key.*)   Open it.
See, I've had it filled with precious relics
To send home to my father – how pleased he'll be!
(*She daydreams a moment then pulls herself together.*)
(*Aside.*) No! No more of that – chase such thoughts away!
(*To CASILDA.*) Fetch me a book to read – oh, I am mad!
Not one word in German – all in Spanish.
The King always hunting – the monotony –
In six months he's spent just twelve days with me!

CASILDA: That is what comes from marrying a king!

(*The QUEEN drifts off again into a reverie, then, with an effort, shakes herself out of it.*)

QUEEN: (*Imperiously.*)
I wish to go out!

(*At these words the DUCHESS, who until now has been sitting motionless on her chair, lifts her head, stands and then curtsies low to the QUEEN.*)

DUCHESS: (*In a dry, clipped tone.*)
                    For the Queen to fare forth,
A lord of Spain with the key to the doors
Must open each one ahead of the Queen;
(*With a contemptuous look at DON GURITAN.*)
But none with that right are here, it would seem.

QUEEN: But I feel I'm behind bars, suffocating!
Duchess, please!

DUCHESS: (*Curtsying again.*) As Camerara Mayor
I but discharge my duty.

QUEEN: (*Despairingly raising her hands to her head, aside.*)
                    Then let me dream!
No!
(*Loud to WOMEN.*)
          Quick, fetch some cards! And a table, too.
We'll play lansquenet!

DUCHESS: (*To WOMEN.*) Kindly stay seated!
(*Rising and curtsying to the QUEEN.*)
The ancient laws state the Queen may play cards
With royalty only or her husband's kin.

QUEEN: (*Angrily.*)
Well, fetch some kinsmen, then!

CASILDA: (*Aside, looking at the DUCHESS.*)
                                        The old stickler!

DUCHESS: (*Making the sign of the cross.*)
I cannot: the last was the late Queen Mother.
God's will it is the King have none other.

QUEEN:
Then something to eat!

CASILDA: Yes! That would be nice.

QUEEN: (*To CASILDA.*)
You can be my guest.

CASILDA: (*Aside, looking at the DUCHESS.*)
                              Bigoted old crone!

DUCHESS: (*Curtsying.*)
When the King's away, the Queen eats alone.
(*Sits.*)

QUEEN: (*In exasperation.*)
Buried alive! – dear God, what shall I do?
I can't go out, can't play, can't eat with whom
I will, just die slowly – it's been one year!

CASILDA: (*Aside and looking compassionately at the QUEEN.*)
Poor lady! Immured daily in this dreary
Dungeon – a flat, stagnant pond at whose edge
She can view at leisure – her sole privilege –
(*Casting a look upstage at DON GURITAN, who is still
standing there motionless.*)
An old, besotted Count who dreams all day
Of the next paltry scrap she might throw his way.

QUEEN:
What can I do? Come, think of something, please!

CASILDA:

I know! When the King's not here, you're in charge:
Summon his ministers to entertain you!

QUEEN: (*Shrugging her shoulders.*)

What pleasure is in that? To have eight rogues
Whining to me of France and her feeble king,
Or of Rome – or the portrait of the Archduke,
Paraded, we hear, through the streets of Burgos
Beneath a canopy of cloth of gold
Borne by four magistrates...no! Something else.

CASILDA:

Well, what if, to brighten your day, I had
Some handsome young squire brought up?

QUEEN: Casilda!

CASILDA:

But, ma'am, I'd so like to see someone young:
This musty old court stifles me to death!
I truly think we age through what we see,
And seeing *old* things speeds senility.

QUEEN:

Silly girl! One day love burns itself out;
It's no sleep that withers, like the earth in drought.
(*Growing pensive.*)
My chief joy is that corner of the park
Where I'm allowed to walk alone.

CASILDA: Oh, yes,

A lovely place! A Garden of Eden
With traps concealed behind every statue!
And of the world there's nothing you can see:
The walls are higher than the tallest tree!

QUEEN:

I'd so love to get out more – once in a while!

CASILDA:

You would? Well, listen, ma'am – keep your voice down –
There's nothing like a dark, gloomy prison
For goading you to search its grey shadows
For that shining jewel called 'The Outer Key' –

I found it! So, whenever you would like
To 'sally forth' and foil these killjoys' plans,
I could easily smuggle you out one night,
Take you on a tour of the city –

QUEEN: Heavens!

CASILDA:
  Well?

QUEEN: Unthinkable! Be quiet!
  (*She moves away from CASILDA and starts to brood again.*)
                                    If only
I were far from all these lords I fear
And in Bavaria with those I love,
Running with my sister across the fields,
Chatting with the peasants who stack the hay!
How sweet those times were! Alas, one evening
This man appeared – he was dressed all in black –
And said – I was holding my sister's hand –
'Madam, you are to be the next Queen of Spain.'
How my father rejoiced! My mother wept.
Both weep now. But I mean to send my father
This box in secret – it will comfort him.
Everything here fills me with despair –
And those pretty birds I brought with me,
All are dead!
(*CASILDA, looking across at the DUCHESS, mimes the wringing of birds' necks.*)
                    They don't allow me flowers
That remind me of home; never do I hear
One word of love, now that I'm Queen of Spain,
In splendour caged – would I were free again!
You were right, the park is a bleak retreat,
The walls so high you scarce can see your feet.
Give me patience!
(*Far off the sound of singing.*)
                    What's that?

CASILDA: The washerwomen
  Singing as they walk back through the heather.

(*The singing gets near enough to distinguish the words. The QUEEN listens eagerly.*)

SONG:

Heed no more the nightingale
Warbling to the moon:
For me you sing a sweeter song
Both night and noon.

The brightest star on a summer's night
I care not if it shine:
Your eyes sparkle twice as bright
Gazing into mine.

Let April deck the gardens fair
With flowers of the very best:
The fairest flower in all the world
Is in your breast.

This flower, this song, these eyes like stars
Brighter than all above,
They make a jewel of priceless worth
Whose name is Love.

(*The voices fade as the washerwomen move away.*)

QUEEN: (*Musing.*)

Love! Ah yes, you happy women – your song
Smells sweet as roses but bears a sharp thorn.

DUCHESS: (*To the other WOMEN.*)

Have someone see those peasant women off!
Their singing vexes the Queen.

QUEEN: (*Quickly.*)   Leave them be!
Besides, you scarce can hear them now, poor souls.
(*To CASILDA, indicating a small window upstage.*)
The trees on this side are planted less thick –
From that window you can see a patch of green:
Perhaps we might catch sight of them –

(*She heads for the window with CASILDA.*)

DUCHESS: (*Rising and curtsying once more.*)   A queen
Of Spain may not look out of windows.

QUEEN: (*She stops and retraces her steps.*)   So –
   The setting sun that floods the land with light,
   The golden haze of dusk before black night,
   Distant voices singing that all may hear
   No more exist for me? Then farewell, dear
   Creation divine! Your wealth I may not see
   Nor even delight in others' liberty.

DUCHESS: (*Signalling to the others to leave.*)
   Out! Today's the Feast of the Holy Apostles.

(*CASILDA starts towards the door. The QUEEN stops her.*)

QUEEN:
   Are you leaving me?

CASILDA: (*Indicating the DUCHESS.*)
                    Marching orders, ma'am.

DUCHESS: (*Curtsying low to the ground.*)
   The Queen must needs be left to her devotions.

(*They all exit after giving the QUEEN low curtsies.*)

QUEEN: (*Alone.*)
   Her devotions? Left more a prey to her dreams!
   How should I escape them, now that I'm alone
   And on a dark road with no lamp by which to see?
   (*Falling into a reverie.*)
   See…yes, that bloody hand-print on the wall!
   He must have been wounded – God! But he has
   Only himself to blame: why should one want
   To climb so high a wall? To bring me flowers
   I am else denied? For that? For so little
   To run such risks, put his life in danger?
   He cut himself on an iron spike – yes,
   A piece of lace was hanging there – one drop
   Of this blood is worth more than all my tears.
   (*Sinking deeper into her reverie.*)
   Every time I go to that bench to see
   If he's left me flowers, I vow to Almighty God,
   This time's the last if He'll make good my lack
   Of will – ' but no: I keep on going back!
   He is hurt! Three days now since he last was there.

Whoever you are, oh shadowy stranger,
You who see me alone so far away
From those who love me, you who ask for nothing,
Nor even hope for aught, come to me now
Heedless of the dangers, you who are ready
To spill your blood, to risk both life and limb
To give the Queen of Spain a simple flower –
Whoever you are, friend, hovering near,
A stern law forbids I feel aught, apart
From wishing you well; but that's from my heart.
(*Presses her hand to her heart.*)
His letter – how it burns me!
(*Falling into a reverie again.*)
                  Then there's the other,
The ruthless don Sallusto – a strange fate
To be pursued by both a sheltering angel
And a hideous creature bred of night!
I see neither; yet they are there, I feel it,
Weaving in and out of my darkest dreams,
Spinning the strands of some trial I must face,
A man who loves me with the other who hates.
Will the first save me from the last? Who knows?
Tossed I am between two winds opposed,
A queen and yet how powerless – queen of naught!
Oh, let me pray!
(*She kneels before the madonna.*)
               Help me, Lady! For shame
I cannot lift my eyes to yours – (*Interrupting herself.*)
                   Oh Heavens,
The lace, the flowers, the letter, they're on fire!
(*Pulling from her bosom a crumpled letter, a bouquet of dried-
up, little blue flowers and a piece of lace stained with blood
which she throws onto the table – then kneeling once more.*)
Holy Virgin, guiding star, heavenly
Queen who giveth the martyr hope, help me –
(*Breaking off.*)
That letter (*Half-turning towards the table.*) draws me like a
    moth to light
(*Kneeling again.*)

But I'll not read it, not again – Gentle
Queen, whom Jesus gave as sister to all those
In need, come to me, I beg you!
(*She rises, goes towards table, stops, then falls on the letter as
if giving in to an irresistible attraction.*)
                                     Once more
But this the last – then I'll have it destroyed.
(*Smiling sadly.*)
How often, now, have I heard myself say that!
(*Unfolds the letter and reads.*)
'Deep in the shadow beneath you is a man
Who loves you; one who, though shrouded in night,
Pines when he sees through that darkness the light
Of a star with whom, poor worm, he's in love;
One who would readily die for you, Ma'am,
Who'd wane to see you wax brilliant above.'
(*Placing the letter on the table.*)
The heart also thirsts and must drink to live
Even though that drink be poison.
(*Returning the letter and lace to her bosom.*)
                             What do I have
In this world? Nothing. I, too, have the right
To love someone! I would have loved the king
Had he wished but no, from him not one word –

(*The great double doors upstage open and the USHER of the
Chamber enters in full dress.*)

USHER: (*In a loud voice.*)
A letter from the King!

QUEEN: (*Joyfully and as if suddenly waking.*)
                         Ah, my prayers were heard!

(*A solemn entrance first of the DUCHESS followed by
CASILDA, the other LADIES-IN-WAITING and DON
GURITAN, then by RUY BLAS, magnificently attired. His
cloak falls over his left arm, hiding it. Two PAGES behind
him, carrying the King's letter on a cushion of cloth of gold,
come forward and kneel before the QUEEN at a respectful
distance.*)

RUY BLAS: (*Aside.*)
Where am I? And why? Ah, she is so fair!

QUEEN: (*Aside.*)
Our Lady, she saved me!
     (*Loud.*) Quick! Give it here!
(*Turning to the portrait of the king.*)
Thank you, sire.
(*To the DUCHESS.*) Where was this letter sent from?

DUCHESS:
From Aranjuez, ma'am. The King is hunting there.

QUEEN: I thank him from the bottom of my soul!
How well he understood my need to hear
A loving word from him, the tedium...
Well? Give it me!

DUCHESS: (*Curtsying and indicating the letter.*)
     Our customs decree
Letters from the King first be read by me.

QUEEN:
Again? Well, read it, then!

(*The DUCHESS takes the letter which she slowly unfolds.*)

CASILDA: (*Aside.*)   A billet doux.

DUCHESS: (*Reading.*)
'It is windy, Ma'am. I have killed six wolves.
Signed, Carlos.'

QUEEN: (*Aside.*) No!

DON GURITAN: (*To the DUCHESS.*) Is that all?

DUCHESS: Yes, my lord.

CASILDA: (*Aside.*)
Six wolves! And windy. News indeed to set
The pulses racing! Feeling unfulfilled?
Bored? Or jealous? Fear not: six wolves he's killed!

DUCHESS: (*Offering the QUEEN the letter.*)
If my Lady would –?

QUEEN: (*Pushing it away.*) No.

CASILDA: (*To the DUCHESS.*) That's really all he wrote?

DUCHESS: Yes. Of course. What needs there any more?
Our King, while still in the thick of the hunt,
Writes what he has killed, describes the weather –
Perfectly correct.
(*Looking at the letter again.*) No, not 'writes' – dictates.

QUEEN: (*Snatching the letter.*)
Not even his hand? Just his signature!
(*Looking at the letter more closely, suddenly freezes.*)
(*Aside.*)
Is this some trick? The hand that wrote these words
Also wrote *my* letter!
(*Touching the letter she has just hidden next to her heart.*)
                        How can this be?
(*To the DUCHESS.*)
Who delivered this – message?

DUCHESS: (*Indicating RUY BLAS.*) He is here.

QUEEN: (*Half-turning towards RUY BLAS.*)
That young man?

DUCHESS: Yes. He brought it in person.
A new equerry it pleases the King
Should now serve you. My lord of Santa Cruz
Recommended him on the King's behalf.

QUEEN:
His name?

DUCHESS: The gentleman's name is Cesar
De Bazan, Count of Garofa, a lord
Of matchless worth to credit his report.

QUEEN:
Good. I'll speak with him.
                (*To RUY BLAS.*) Sir –

RUY BLAS: (*Aside and trembling.*)   She spoke – to me,
Looks – at me – Stop your shaking!

DUCHESS: Draw near, Count.

DON GURITAN: (*Aside, scowling at RUY BLAS.*)
    This young equerry could steal my thunder.

    (*A troubled RUY BLAS approaches the QUEEN slowly.*)

QUEEN: (*To RUY BLAS.*)
    Have you come from Aranjuez?

RUY BLAS: (*Bowing.*)   I have, ma'am.

QUEEN:
    The King is well?
    (*RUY BLAS bows.*)
    (*Indicating the letter.*) And he dictated this?

RUY BLAS:
    He was on horseback and dictated it – (*Hesitating.*)
    To one of his assistants.

QUEEN: (*Aside.*)   I dare not ask
    Which one – his eyes are so strangely piercing!
    (*Aloud.*) Good. You may go.
    (*RUY BLAS turns to go.*)   Were – many lords with him?
    (*Aside.*) Why does this young man's bearing move me so?

    (*RUY BLAS, who has started to walk away, now returns to
    the QUEEN and inclines his head in the affirmative.*)

    Which ones?

RUY BLAS: I'm ignorant of their names, Ma'am:
    In all I was there for just a short while,
    Having left Madrid but three days ago.

QUEEN: (*Aside.*)
    Three days!

    (*She stares at RUY BLAS, deeply troubled.*)

RUY BLAS: (*Aside.*) She belongs to another! Oh,
    Back, jealousy, back to your lair below!

DON GURITAN: (*Approaching RUY BLAS.*)
    The Queen's equerry, are we? I'll be brief:
    You know your tasks? – Well, tonight you'll attend
    In the room next door, so, should the King come
    To… call on his wife, *you* can let him in.

RUY BLAS: (*Aside and trembling.*)
 I? Let in the King! (*Aloud.*) But the King's away.

DON GURITAN:
 And might return – on impulse – who can say?

RUY BLAS: (*Aside.*)
 No!

DON GURITAN: (*Aside.*)
  What's wrong with the fellow?

QUEEN: (*Having overheard and observed this exchange, aside.*)
          How pale he's grown!

(*RUY BLAS sways slightly and supports himself on the arm
of a chair.*)

CASILDA:
 The young man's not well!

RUY BLAS: (*Barely able to stand.*) No – it must be the heat –
 Strange how – the sun beat down – the journey – long –
 (*Aside.*)
 Let in the King!

(*RUY BLAS collapses onto the chair. His cloak falls aside
revealing his left hand wrapped in a blood-stained bandage.*)

CASILDA: Oh, great Heavens, ma'am! Look!
 He is hurt!

QUEEN: Hurt –

CASILDA: His hand – I think he's fainted.
 Quick! Give him something to help bring him round!

QUEEN: (*Searching in her gorget.*)
 I have some liquid here in a phial which –
 (*Aside, seeing the lace cuff on RUY BLAS's right wrist.*)
 His lace – it's the same!

(*As she takes out the phial from her bosom, in her confusion
the QUEEN pulls out at the same time the piece of
bloodstained lace which she had hidden there and which now
falls to the ground. RUY BLAS, whose eyes have never left
the QUEEN's face, witnesses this. Their eyes meet and there
is a silence.*)

(*Aside.*) It's him!

RUY BLAS: (*Aside.*) Next to her heart –

QUEEN: (*Aside.*)
It's him!

RUY BLAS: (*Aside.*) Dear God, if I were now to die – !

(*No-one, in the hubbub that comes from all the LADIES clustering round RUY BLAS, notices what passes between him and the QUEEN.*)

CASILDA: (*Making RUY BLAS inhale from the phial.*)
How did you come to hurt yourself? Just now?
(*RUY BLAS shakes his head.*)
An old wound, then, your ride here reopened?
Then why make you bring a letter all that way?

QUEEN: So many questions! Have you finished yet?

DUCHESS: (*To CASILDA.*)
What does all this have to do with the Queen?

QUEEN: He brought the letter for the simple reason
He was the one who wrote it.

CASILDA: He didn't say
He did.

QUEEN: (*Momentarily caught out, then recovering herself.*)
Hold your tongue!

CASILDA: (*To RUY BLAS.*) Do you feel better?

RUY BLAS:
I feel reborn.

QUEEN: (*To her women.*) Come, it's time to go in.
Let the Count be shown where he is to lodge.
(*To the pages but for the benefit of RUY BLAS.*)
The King, as you know, won't be here tonight:
He hunts – and the season is at its height.

(*The QUEEN exits with her retinue.*)

CASILDA: (*Looking after the QUEEN.*)
The Queen is acting strangely.

(CASILDA takes the casket of relics and exits after the QUEEN, leaving RUY BLAS alone on stage. He appears to be in the grips of a dream. He picks up the piece of lace, looks at it and then kisses it.)

RUY BLAS: Dear God, please
Keep me from madness!
(Looking at the lace.)   It was next to her heart!

(He hides it in his tunic. DON GURITAN enters from the door through which he followed the QUEEN. He walks slowly towards RUY BLAS. Coming up close to him and without saying a word, he half draws his sword, measuring it with his eye against that of RUY BLAS. They are not the same length. He sheathes his sword. RUY BLAS looks at him astonished.)

DON GURITAN:
I will fetch two that are of equal length.

RUY BLAS:
What do you mean, sir?

DON GURITAN: *(Solemnly.)* In the year sixteen fifty
I lost my heart – in Alicante it was.
A young man there of pleasing appearance,
A prince of peacocks, would eye my mistress
Brazenly, strut beneath her balcony
As bold as brass, his feathers on display.
Vasquez, his name, bastard son of some lord –
I killed him.
(RUY BLAS goes to speak but DON GURITAN holds up a hand to stop him.)
                        Some time later – that would be
Sixty-five, sixty-six – a certain Gil,
Count of Iscola, a fine cavalier,
Sent a slave called Grifel de Viserta
With a billet doux to my beloved's house.
She – Angelica so called – showed me the same:
Both slave and master I killed in her name.

RUY BLAS:
Sir!

DON GURITAN: Later still, towards sixteen eighty,
 I had cause to believe my love, a coquette
 Easily led, was deceiving me with one
 Tirso Gamonal, a handsome young lad
 Whose sweetly sneering face perfectly matched
 His dashing air – I'm sure you know the type;
 'Twas then the vogue to shoe one's mules with gold.
 I killed don Tirso Gamonal.

RUY BLAS: But, sir,
 What should all this mean?

DON GURITAN: It means, my dear Count,
 Buckets drawn from wells tend to hold water;
 That tomorrow the sun will rise at four;
 That I know a spot off the beaten track,
 Made for men of mettle, behind the church;
 That you, if I heard right, are called Cesar,
 I, Don Gaspar Guritan y Guervarra.

RUY BLAS: (*Coldly.*)
 Very good, sir, I will be there.

 (*CASILDA meantime has crept in out of curiosity by the
 small upstage door and overheard the last exchange unseen.*)

CASILDA: A duel!
 I must warn the Queen. (*Exits.*)

DON GURITAN: (*Continuing doggedly.*)
       Please you, sir, to learn
 The kind of man I am – I'll put you to school
 And say that never was I much enamoured
 Of these popinjays, these whisker-curling
 Fops of fashion the ladies so adore
 Who change from sour to sweet with protean speed,
 Make spaniel eyes across the room and strike
 Graceful poses against the arms of chairs,
 Swooning at mere scratches. Transparent snares!

RUY BLAS:
 I don't follow you.

DON GURITAN: Sir, you tread on my heels!
 We have our eyes on one and the same treasure

And this palace cannot contain us both.
You as equerry, I as chief steward
Have equal rights but you, sir, have the edge:
We do not balance in the scales for where I
Have the elder's rights, you have the younger's
Which makes me afeard: I see across that board
Where I sit and starve a ravenous youth
With tiger's teeth and flashing eyes who wears
The victor's bays and this I cannot brook.
As to competing on Love's jousting field
I have not the requisite verbal frills.
Besides, I have the gout, and, furthermore,
Am not so foolish as to enter the lists
For any Penelope's heart as prize
Against a master of fainting fits and sighs.
Thus, in view of looks winsome and demure,
Your bearing, youth and evident allure,
I'm obliged to kill you.

RUY BLAS: Well, you'll have to try.

DON GURITAN:

Count of Garofa, tomorrow at dawn
At the aforesaid place and quite alone
Armed like gentlemen with sword and poniard
We'll fight to the death like the noblemen we are.

(*Offering his hand to RUY BLAS who takes it.*)

RUY BLAS:

Not a word of this?
(*DON GURITAN signals his agreement.*)
                         Till tomorrow, then.

(*RUY BLAS exits.*)

DON GURITAN: (*Alone.*)

A firm hand and steady, this gentleman –
To know he's bound to die and to show no fear
Proclaims he has courage –
(*Hearing a key turning in the door to the QUEEN's
bedchamber, DON GURITAN turns round.*)
                         But whom have we here?

214

(*The QUEEN enters and approaches DON GURITAN with some zest. He is both surprised and delighted to see her. She is carrying the little casket of relics.*)

QUEEN: (*Smiling.*)
  The very man I wanted!

DON GURITAN: (*Overjoyed.*) To what, ma'am,
  Do I owe this honour?

QUEEN: (*Placing casket on small table.*) It's a trifle, sir.
  (*Laughing.*)
  We were talking just now – women, you know –
  And Casilda said – amongst other things –
  Well, *she* maintained you would perform for me
  Anything I asked.

DON GURITAN: She was right!

QUEEN: Gracious me!
  I maintained you wouldn't.

DON GURITAN: You were wrong, ma'am!

QUEEN:
  She said for me you'd render life and limb –

DON GURITAN:
  She did well to speak of me so.

QUEEN: I said
  You would not.

DON GURITAN: And I say I would! For you,
  Your Majesty, I would do anything.

QUEEN:
  Anything?

DON GURITAN: Anything!

QUEEN: Well, then, let me see –
  Swear that whatever I say you'll do it now.

DON GURITAN:
  By Caspar the King, my patron saint, I vow
  To obey your command, may I rot else in hell!

QUEEN: (*Taking up the casket.*)
    Good. Bid Madrid, then, an instant farewell
    And take this box made of wood of aloes
    To the Elector of Neubourg, my dear father.

DON GURITAN:(*Aside.*)
    I've been gulled! (*Aloud.*) To Neubourg!

QUEEN: Yes, sir, Neubourg.

DON GURITAN:
    Six hundred leagues!

QUEEN: Five hundred and fifty.
    (*Indicating the silk cover in which the casket is wrapped.*)
    Take great care that this blue fringe does not fade
    On the journey.

DON GURITAN: When do I leave?

QUEEN: Now, of course.

DON GURITAN:
    Ah! Not tomorrow?

QUEEN: Out of the question.

DON GURITAN: (*Aside.*)
    Gulled, oh gulled!
    (*Aloud.*)   But –

QUEEN: Now!

DON GURITAN: What – ?

QUEEN: You gave your word.

DON GURITAN:
    There's this matter –

QUEEN: Impossible.

DON GURITAN: So slight
    A thing –

QUEEN: Hurry!

DON GURITAN: One day!

QUEEN: Not a moment!

DON GURITAN:
    For –

QUEEN: Do my bidding.

DON GURITAN:　　　　　I –

QUEEN:　　　　　　　　　No.

DON GURITAN:　　　　　　　But –

QUEEN:　　　　　　　　　　　　Go now!

DON GURITAN:　　　　　　　　　　If –

QUEEN:

Look, dear Count, I'll seal it with a kiss!

(*Throwing her arms about DON GURITAN's neck, the QUEEN then kisses him.*)

DON GURITAN: (*Torn between frustration and delight.*)
You have disarmed me, ma'am. I will obey.
(*Aside.*) Man has his will but Woman has her way.

QUEEN: (*Indicating the window.*)
A carriage is below, ready and waiting.

DON GURITAN: (*Aside.*)
She foresaw it all!
(*He hurriedly writes a few words on a piece of paper and rings a bell. A page enters.*)
(*Aloud.*)　　　　　　　Page, take this letter
Instantly to don Cesar de Bazan. (*Page exits.*)
(*Aside.*)
This duel must be postponed till I return –
Which I will!
(*Aloud.*)　　　　To make you happy, ma'am,
I take my leave.

QUEEN:　　　　　Good.
(*DON GURITAN takes up the casket, kisses the QUEEN's hand, bows deeply and exits. A moment later the sound of a departing carriage is heard. The QUEEN falls with relief into an armchair.*)
　　　　　　　　　　He will come to no harm!

End of Act Two

ACT THREE

(Ruy Blas)

The Council Chamber of the King's Palace in Madrid. Upstage a large door above some steps. Left, in an angle, a cant is closed off by a high warp tapestry. In the angle opposite there is a window. To the right, a square table covered with a green velvet cloth around which are ranged stools for eight or ten persons corresponding to the number of desks placed on the table. At the side of the table facing the audience is a large armchair covered with cloth of gold and having a canopy, also of cloth, of gold emblazoned with the arms of Spain and the royal crown. There is a chair to one side of this.

The King's Privy Council is about to meet. This Council consists of: DON MANUEL Arias, President of Castille; Don Pedro Velez de Guevarra, Count of CAMPOREAL and Councillor of the Privy Purse; Don Fernando de Cordova y Aguilar, Marquess of PRIEGO and of the same standing; Antonio UBILLA, Chief Secretary of the Treasury; MONTAZGO, Councillor of the Robe of the Chamber of the Indies; and COVADENGA, Chief Secretary for the Balearic and Canary Isles. Several other Councillors in court dress or, if of the Robe, in black. CAMPOREAL wears the cross of Calatrava on his cloak. Around his neck PRIEGO wears the Golden Fleece. DON MANUEL and the Count of CAMPOREAL are talking together with lowered voices downstage. The other Privy Councillors are clustered in groups about the Chamber.

DON MANUEL:
  There's more to such good fortune than meets the eye.

CAMPOREAL:
  He wears the Golden Fleece, he's Secretary
  Both of State and Council, Chief Minister,
  Now Duke of Olmedo – !

DON MANUEL: And all in only
  Six months!

CAMPOREAL: Never without some hidden hand.

DON MANUEL: (*Mysteriously.*)   The Queen!

CAMPOREAL:
Sick and deranged, the King – whose heart
In truth lies in the tomb of his first wife –
Immures himself in the Escurial
Ceding to this Queen all the reins of power.

DON MANUEL:
We are her horse. But she is don Cesar's.

CAMPOREAL:
But with the life he leads! So unnatural!
The Queen, first: you know he never sees her?
Indeed it seems that they avoid each other…
It's true! I know for sure: for six months now
I've had them watched. Then, near the Hotel Tormez
There's this house which has the look of the blind,
Its shutters always closed: it's there he lives –
Or hides rather – whenever the mood takes him,
While two black servants stand guard night and day
Who, if they weren't dumb, might have much to say.

DON MANUEL:
Dumb?

CAMPOREAL: They are mutes. The rest of his servants
Live in the palace, his official abode.

DON MANUEL:
How strange!

UBILLA:(*Having joined them some moments before.*)
                    He's of noble stock. That's for sure.

CAMPOREAL: (*Sneering, to DON MANUEL.*)
Stranger still how he plays at being pure.
(*Turning to UBILLA.*)
Santa-Cruz spoke up for him, too: cousins
Both to that Marquess Sallusto – (*Pointedly.*)
                    – who fell last year?
There was a time when this our present master
Was the greatest of fools beneath the moon!
One fine day – and this from those who knew him –

This clown began to fritter away his wealth –
New wench, new carriage, for each day of the week –
Devising such schemes to make his fortune fly,
One year and he'd have sucked Peru bone dry!
Then, he was gone – but where to? None could say.

DON MANUEL:
So the fool's grown wise – grown teeth, too, to bite us.

CAMPOREAL:
Women, loose once, when withered, grow self-righteous.

UBILLA:
I think the man honest.

CAMPOREAL: (*Laughing.*) Oh, Ubilla, how
Naive you are to let his halo blind you!
(*In an insinuating tone.*)
The Queen's household, civil and ordinary,
(*Consulting figures.*)
Costs six hundred and sixty-four thousand
And sixty-six ducats a year – a flood of which
Midas himself would be proud! Cast your net
And rest assured: 'Bait the water, catch the fish'?

PRIEGO: (*Having approached.*)
Come, come! And it not displease you, good sirs,
I deem your words unwise, your policy rash:
My late grandfather, who grew up alongside
The Duke of San-Lucar, would often advise:
'Snap at the King's heels but lick his favourite's hand.'
Now, gentlemen, let's to the affairs of state!

(*Everyone takes his seat around the table. Some take up pens, others shuffle papers, the rest sit about idly. There is a brief silence.*)

MONTAZGO: (*Low to UBILLA.*)
What of that request of mine for money
From the relics fund to buy my nephew
The post of judge?

UBILLA: (*Low to MONTAZGO.*) You, what of your promise
To name my cousin, Melchior of Elva,

Magistrate of the Ebro?

MONTAZGO: (*Protesting.*) We did but of late
Dower your daughter! *And* her wedding feast
Continues yet! These incessant demands...

UBILLA:
You'll have your judge.

MONTAZGO: And you your magistrate.

(*They shake hands.*)

COVADENGA: (*Rising.*)
Gentlemen and Councillors of Castille,
To ensure each remain within his own sphere,
It behoves us to agree our several rights
And make just division accordingly.
It were a sin against the public weal
That Spain's great wealth be scattered far and wide
But some have too little, others too much.
Levies on tobacco are yours, Ubilla;
Indigo and musk, Marquess of Priego;
Camporeal collects the army levy,
The export tax, salt-tax and a thousand more:
The five per cent on gold, on amber, jet –
(*To MONTAZGO.*)
You who look on me with such troubled mien,
You have skilfully hoarded for yourself
The arsenic tax and rights to snow, then there's
Dry passage toll, tax on playing cards, brass,
Fines paid in lieu of flogging, the ocean tithes,
The tax on lead, rosewood – shall I go on? –
Sirs, grant me *some* share of this – I have none!

CAMPOREAL: (*Bursting out with laughter.*)
The old devil! Compared to him we're paupers:
Quite apart from the Indies, he spreads his wings
Across the two seas: he has the Isles in fief,
Majorca in one claw, in t'other Tenerife!

COVADENGA: (*Growing angry.*)
I said I had none!

PRIEGO: (*Laughing.*) Don't forget the slaves!

(*All rise and start speaking at the same time, squabbling amongst themselves.*)

MONTAZGO:

The forest rights! My claim's long overdue!

COVADENGA: (*To PRIEGO.*)

See I get the arsenic and the slaves are yours!

(*RUY BLAS has meantime entered from the upstage door and been an unobserved witness of the above scene. He is dressed in black velvet with a scarlet velvet cloak, has a white feather in his hat and the Golden Fleece around his neck. After listening to them in silence, he now suddenly comes downstage slowly, appearing in the midst of them at the height of their quarrelling.*)

RUY BLAS:

May I join in the feast?

(*All turn and there is a shocked and uneasy silence. RUY BLAS puts on his hat and continues whilst gazing at each one in turn.*)

                    Good Councillors!
Upright Ministers! Is this how you serve Spain?
Servants turned looters? Have you no shame –
And at this dark hour when Spain lies bowed
And bleeding – to have minds bent alone on how
To fill your pockets and flee – like Jezebels?
Robbers, I brand you, of the grave you yourselves
Have dug for the corpse of this, your country!
Yes, corpse! For see – we *can* see, can't we? –
How Spain's glory, her greatness turns to dust!
Since the reign of Phillip the Fourth we have lost
Portugal and Brazil unopposed – not a word! –
Brisach in Alsace, Steinfort in Luxembourg,
The Franche-Comté, Roussillon and Goa,
Hormuz, five leagues of coastline, Pernambuco
And, with the Lowlands, the Blue Mountain range!
Behold us, too, from east to west disdained –
Laughed at by Europe where the English and Dutch

Cast lots who's to take what's left and how much,
As if the King were already in his grave!
Rome smiles and sniggers; in Piedmont you are brave
Indeed to station more than a handful of men;
Though an ally, Savoy's a treacherous den
Of rogues, not least her Duke; France, a hyena
Biding its time; Austria, too, a gleam of
Teeth in the dark; while the heir designate,
The Bavarian prince, hovers close to death.
Then we have the Viceroys: Medina, first,
Whose lust's the talk of Naples; Vaudemont's worse:
Milan's up for sale! While Legañez, too,
Would lose us Flanders. But what is there to do
When the State is destitute, ruined, drained
Of both money and men? On the Spanish Main
God in His anger has seen fit to allow
The loss of three hundred ships, that without
Counting galleys – and you dare...! Imagine, sirs,
In twenty years the people – I have the figures –
Bent double beneath the huge load they've borne,
The wretched people, on whom you pile more
To pay for your pleasures, you've sweated all told
Of four hundred and thirty millions in gold!
But still that's not enough, my masters, no,
Still more you'd have – the shame I feel is – oh,
I burn for you! – And everywhere roam mobs
Of lawless mercenaries who fire our crops,
Aim their cannon from every bush – and, just
As if civil war were raging, knives are thrust
Into every hand: monk fights monk! neighbours
Feud; each man preys on the next – God save us! –
A cannibal crew round a doomed ship's mast.
The Church crumbles and the cracks sprout grass
Alive with adders; greatness is a case
Of birth, not deeds; intrigue usurps good faith.
Spain is a cess-pit into which has poured
The filth of other nations: there's no lord
Without his hundred cut-throats gabbling like geese

In a hundred tongues – Flemish, Genoese,
Sardinian – Babel has come to Madrid.
The law glares at the poor, smiles on the rich;
At night you can hear murder victims cry
For help – last night I was robbed, even I! –
Half of Madrid by the other half is plagued,
Her judges all corrupt, soldiers unpaid,
Men who once conquered the world I'd now put
At barely six thousand and these go barefoot:
Ragged gangs of rustics armed with knives
Who ply a double trade, dropping all pretence
To be soldiers, come night, to rob and terrorize –
Matalobos musters a greater strength
Than any lord: a thief makes war on the King
Of Spain! – at whose passing carriage peasants fling
Insults, while he, your lord, consumed with grief
And fear, sits in the Escurial – beneath
His feet only the dead for company –
And broods on the empire's dying agony!
Spain, whose imperial pinions Europe has clipped,
Ungainly hops where once she soared, stripped
Of her plumes, gone all her pinnacled domains –
Yet here you wrangle over what remains!
The Spanish people, on whose backs you've grown tall –
Once so great, now wasted piteous small –
Slinks like a sick and flea-infested lion
Into the darkness of a cave to die in.
Oh mighty Emperor, Carlos the Fifth,
How can you sleep at such an hour as this
There in your tomb? At such a time of shame?
Rise up and see how the worst have laid claim
To what the best once held, how this awesome edifice
Of imperial stones hangs over an abyss!
Come, Carlos, come to our aid, we need your strength
For Spain is dying – come to her defence!
The imperial orb you held in your right hand,
Which shone so bright that Spain was thought the land
Where the sun rises, is now more like the moon,

A waning light, three quarters gnawed and soon
To be swallowed by another nation's dawn.
Your golden legacy's been loaded up and borne
To the market-place to be fingered and exchanged
For cash – And can you sleep, your sceptre profaned,
Weighed for its worth, your royal purple cut
Into doublets in which crookbacked dwarfs now strut?

(*The COUNCILLORS are dismayed and silent. The only heads not lowered are those of the Marquess of PRIEGO and the Count of CAMPOREAL who glare angrily at RUY BLAS. CAMPOREAL then speaks to PRIEGO, goes to the table and writes some words on a piece of paper which both he and the Marquess then sign.*)

CAMPOREAL: (*Indicating PRIEGO and presenting the paper to RUY BLAS.*)

Here in writing are both our resignations –
Your Grace.

RUY BLAS: (*Coldly and taking the paper.*)
⠀⠀⠀⠀⠀⠀Thank you. You will withdraw, each to his
Own estates and along with family,
You – (*To PRIEGO.*) to Andalusia, and you, Count –
(*To CAMPOREAL.*) To Castille. I want you gone tomorrow.

(*The two lords bow stiffly and, with their hats on, haughtily quit the Chamber. RUY BLAS turns to the others.*)

Any unwilling to tread the selfsame road
As mine should follow these two gentlemen.

(*No-one speaks. RUY BLAS seats himself on a high-backed chair at the table to the right of the royal chair and busies himself with opening letters. While he peruses these, COVADENGA, DON MANUEL and UBILLA converse in low voices.*)

UBILLA:(*To COVADENGA, indicating RUY BLAS.*)
Young sir, we have a master! A man destined
For greatness.

DON MANUEL: Yes – *if* he's given the chance.

COVADENGA:

And softens somewhat this moralistic stance.

UBILLA:

A new Richelieu!

DON MANUEL: Or a Duke of San-Lucar.

RUY BLAS: (*Having just read a letter with mounting concern.*)
     What's this? More intrigues? Do you hear, my masters?
     (*Reading.*) 'Duke of Olmedo, beware: there is a plot
     Afoot to entrap and bring about the downfall
     Of someone of high standing in Madrid.'
     They don't say whom. I will indeed beware.
     The letter's anonymous.
     (*A Court USHER enters, approaches RUY BLAS and bows deeply.*)
                         Well? What is it?

USHER: The ambassador of France craves audience
     With your Excellency.

RUY BLAS: D'Harcourt? – No, not now.

USHER: (*Bowing.*)
     My lord, the Imperial Nuncio awaits
     Your Excellency in the guests' chamber.

RUY BLAS:

     At this hour of the day? Out of the question.

     (*The USHER bows and exits. A PAGE, who entered a few moments earlier, now approaches RUY BLAS. He is dressed in bright red livery with silver braid.*)

     (*To the PAGE, on seeing him.*)
     I'm a ghost, page, invisible to all.

PAGE: (*Low.*)
     Count Guritan, who is returned from Neubourg –

RUY BLAS:

     Ah! – Tell him where my house is. If he wants,
     He may see me there tomorrow – tell him that.
     (*The PAGE exits. RUY BLAS turns to the Councillors.*)

Our business, gentlemen, will have to wait:
Please you to return in two hours.

(*Everyone leaves after bowing deeply to RUY BLAS. Alone, he walks back and forth, buried in his thoughts. All at once, the tapestry in the corner of the room is pushed aside and the QUEEN appears. Dressed in white and wearing a crown, she seems to radiate joy and gazes at RUY BLAS with both admiration and respect. Behind the arm with which she holds up the tapestry a dark recess can be glimpsed and at its back a door. Turning round, RUY BLAS sees the QUEEN and is for a moment paralysed as if before a vision.*)

QUEEN: My thanks!

RUY BLAS:
Heavens!

QUEEN: To address them as you did was well done!
No longer, duke, can I curb my strong desire
To press the hand of one I so admire!
(*Moving swiftly to RUY BLAS, she takes his hand before he can prevent it.*)

RUY BLAS: (*Breaking from her, aside.*)
To see her now after so long a fast!
(*Loud and going to recess.*)
You were in there – ?

QUEEN: Yes, and heard everything.
I sat and drank in every single word!

RUY BLAS:
I had no idea – So this little room – (*Pointing to the recess.*)

QUEEN:
A secret recess hewn out of the wall
By Philip the Third from where, like some ghost,
He could hear unseen all his nobles said.
Carlos the Second has hidden there as well,
Slumped in misery, listening with dread
As they loot his land for what they can sell.

RUY BLAS:
What did he say?

QUEEN: He said nothing.

RUY BLAS: Nothing?
What did he do?

QUEEN: What he did? He went hunting.
But you – even now your voice rings in my ears,
Cowing those lords, treating them with disdain –
How true what you said! How gloriously true!
I lifted up the edge of the tapestry
And saw you, saw your eyes, hot with noble rage,
Rain down lightning on their heads as you spoke,
Fell them like rotten trees, till you alone stood!
But how do you come to know all you do
And can see behind the world's outward show?
You seem omniscient! And the way you spoke –
Why did your voice sound like that of a king?
And why did I think I saw some god above you,
Awesome and tall?

RUY BLAS: Why? Because I love you!
Because these vandals, who loathe me to a man,
Could bring Spain's roof crashing down on *your* head!
Because my love for you leaves no room for fear:
To save you, I'd save not just Spain but the world!
Unhappy wretch, when I think of you I feel
Like the blind must feel when they think of the sun,
Such is my love. My dreams are all of you.
Listen, Ma'am: from afar, from the shadows below,
I have loved you and – though I'd not so much as dare
Touch the tip of your finger – have hurt my eyes
By too long gazing on your angelic light!
The pain I have endured, if you but knew –
I speak to you now, but for six long months
I've hid my love, hid from you, and the price
I've paid…! Those men are of no concern to me –
I love you!… God! that I should dare to say so
To your Majesty's face! Forgive me! tell me
What to do – if to die, I will! Oh, I fear
I have offended you –

QUEEN: Oh, don't stop, my dear
   Lord! No-one ever has said such things to me
   Before! I hear you speak and my soul takes wing
   And soars, held aloft by your voice, your gaze –
   Oh, it's I who have suffered – if you but knew –
   A hundred times over the last six months
   When your eyes avoided mine…but stop, my tongue
   Prattles on – so bold! – I should be shyer –

RUY BLAS: (*Who has been drinking in her every word.*)
   No, don't stop! The joy your words inspire – !

QUEEN: Listen, then – (*Raising her eyes to heaven and reverting
   to the soliloquising her loneliness has accustomed her to.*)
                – yes, I'll tell him everything:
   If a crime, I care not! When the heart within
   Is cleft, its stored-up secrets speak out loud –
   So you've hid from your queen? She has sought you out!
   I come here – (*Pointing to recess.*) every day, have overheard
   And silently absorbed your every word,
   Watched you deliberate, decide – so enthralled
   That I felt you were he who should be called
   The rightful king, your voice so inspired me!
   For six months now it is I who have slyly
   Seen to your advancement – perhaps you knew? –
   A woman has done what God failed to do!
   You have my respect – yes, and all your care
   Has been for my good: once that was a flower,
   Now it is an empire you lay at my feet!
   Virtuous first, I now behold you great –
   (*Turning away.*) This the way that a woman's heart is won!
   And if I err, tell me why, like some nun,
   Was I ever locked away in this dark cell,
   Deprived of love, of hope – an earthly hell?
   (*Turning back.*) One day when we have time I'll tell you all
   I've suffered – no-one ever I could call
   On – humiliated every time I protest –
   Why, only yesterday…listen, I detest
   My room – you who are so wise will know
   How sad some rooms can make you feel – and so

I wished to change. The queen! But would they let her?
No! I'm caged. A lackey's treated better!
You, my lord duke, have been sent here by Heaven
To save the tottering state, relieve the oppression
Of those who toil, the suffering of their queen:
To love her, yes! And though these words may seem
Disordered, wild, believe them: they are true.

RUY BLAS: (*Falling to his knees.*)
My lady –

QUEEN: (*Gravely.*) Listen, don Cesar, to you
I give my heart. Though queen for all others,
For you I'm a woman who in the name of love is
Wholly yours. My honour you'll not betray:
Send for me and I'll come, be it night or day.
Cesar, be proud: within you is *your* throne,
Your mind your crown, and one that's yours alone.
(*She kisses RUY BLAS on the forehead.*)
Farewell.
(*She lifts the tapestry and disappears.*)

RUY BLAS: (*Absorbed as if in the contemplation of an angel.*)
        Heaven opens before my gaze!
This, dear God, is the moment of my birth.
A world of light, the paradise of dreams,
Floods my soul with a living radiance!
Everywhere – within me, without – there's joy
Unbounded, mystery, intoxication,
Pride and all that here on earth comes nearest
To the Divine: Love enthroned in glory!
The queen loves me! Yes, me! Dear God, it's true
And this truth makes me greater than the king –
My mind reels! To have won her, won her love –
What joy! Duke of Olmedo – Spain at my feet –
Her heart mine, this angel I adore – she speaks
And suddenly I am more than just a man.
I dreamt this Heaven yet live it now awake
For yes, it *was* she who spoke to me, I'm sure:
She wore a diadem of silver lace

And, while she spoke, I saw – and see it still –
On her gold bracelet an eagle engraved.
She trusts me. She told me so, the poor angel!
And if it's true that through the gift of love
God sought to bind in mutual accord
What spurs us to greatness with what moves our hearts,
Then I who fear nothing, now I have her love,
I who through her favour wield total power,
I whose swelling heart kings might well envy! –
Boldly declare with God as my witness
That yes, my lady, you may trust me indeed,
As Queen my strength, as a woman my heart!
Fear not: nothing could my pure love deter
From serving you faithfully…

(*In the meantime a man has entered by the upstage door,
wrapped in a large cloak and with a hat gallooned in silver.
Unseen by RUY BLAS, and at the moment when the latter,
quite out of himself with happiness, raises his eyes to heaven,
this man swiftly places his hand on RUY BLAS' shoulder.
With a start, as if waking from a dream, RUY BLAS turns.
The man lets his cloak fall open and RUY BLAS recognises
DON SALLUSTO, who is dressed in the same livery as RUY
BLAS' page had been earlier.*)

DON SALLUSTO: (*Laying his hand on RUY BLAS' shoulder.*)
                              Greetings, fine sir!

RUY BLAS: (*Aside, appalled.*)
  Good God! The marquess – all is lost!

DON SALLUSTO: (*Smiling.*)   I'll wager
  You weren't thinking of me.

RUY BLAS: Indeed, my lord,
  You did – surprise me.
    (*Aside.*)   Night again! The sun fled:
  I looked for an angel – a devil came instead.

(*He moves swiftly to the tapestry hiding the secret recess and
bolts the little door. He then returns to DON SALLUSTO in
an agitated state.*)

DON SALLUSTO:

Well, and how are things?

RUY BLAS: (*Staring blankly at the impassive DON SALLUSTO and as if barely able to collect his thoughts.*)

Why this livery?

DON SALLUSTO: (*Continuing to smile.*)

I needed to obtain entrance to the palace.
Dressed like this, I can move about at will –
I chose yours. It suits me well – don't you think?
(*He puts on his hat. RUY BLAS remains bare-headed.*)

RUY BLAS:

But I fear for you –

DON SALLUSTO: Fear? Don't make me laugh!

RUY BLAS:

You are exiled.

DON SALLUSTO: Am I? Yes, possibly.

RUY BLAS:

Here in the palace – and in broad daylight –
What if you were recognised?

DON SALLUSTO: What courtier

Would waste precious moments of his happy life
Trying to put a name to a banished face?
Besides, who looks twice at a lackey's, I ask you?
(*DON SALLUSTO sits in an armchair, RUY BLAS remains standing.*)
And what's the talk here in Madrid? Is it true
That, in an overblown blaze of zeal
And all for the sake of the public weal,
You've exiled dear Priego, a grandee no less?
It must have slipped your mind that you're related:
His mother's a Sandoval. Like yours, damn it!
Gold on a sable stripe, their coat of arms? –
There, look on yours, Cesar – no mistaking.
Not the done thing, dear boy, not with relations.
Dog eat dog? That's no way to get to Heaven.
Birds of a feather, you know? Damn the crows!
Look after number one.

RUY BLAS: (*Growing more composed.*) Nevertheless,
Sir, if you'll permit, Priego as minister
Should have served Spain, not added to her ills.
An army must be raised but there's no money;
The Bavarian heir will die very soon;
And the Count of Harrach, whom you know, told me
Yesterday his master, the emperor,
Had warned, if the Archduke were to press his claim,
War would break out –

DON SALLUSTO: I find it rather cold
In here – be a good man and close the window.

(*Wincing under the humiliation, RUY BLAS hesitates a
moment, then, making an effort, goes slowly towards the
window, closes it and returns to DON SALLUSTO who,
still seated in the armchair, watches him coldly.*)

RUY BLAS: (*Resuming his attempt to convince DON SALLUSTO.*)
I beg you, think how hard a war would prove –
And with no money – ? Listen, my lord, Spain's
Salvation depends on *our* keeping faith.
I for one have let the emperor know –
Bluffing we could put an army in the field –
I'd fight him tooth and nail...

DON SALLUSTO: (*Interrupting RUY BLAS and indicating the
handkerchief he had dropped on his entrance.*)
                        Excuse me. Kindly
Pick up my handkerchief.
(*As if undergoing torture, RUY BLAS again hesitates, then,
stooping, picks up the handkerchief. He gives it to DON
SALLUSTO who puts it in his pocket.*)
                        You were saying?

RUY BLAS: (*With an effort.*)
Spain's salvation, her fate, is in our hands
Which demands we set aside all self-interest.
How the people would bless their deliverer!
Save them with me! Let's be equal to the hour,
Expose the whispering schemers, unmask the rogues –

DON SALLUSTO: (*Nonchalantly.*)
    All this I find less than entertaining –
    It reeks rather of the pedant's one gift
    For braying loud on any theme he will.
    A paltry million most of which is spent
    Merits such a rumpus? A great lord, dear boy,
    Is not your boorish bigot; the life he leads
    Is more…expansive. Note, *I* do not rant,
    While you, fine sir, who'd set the world to rights,
    Look fit to burst with apoplectic pride!
    To be the people's darling, is that your goal?
    Peasants and greasy tradesmen licking your hand?
    Most diverting! But hardly very novel.
    Popularity? Nothing but fool's gold
    Won by yapping at tax-collectors' doors –
    Charming, but I can think of better employment.
    'Set aside self-interest'? What on earth for?
    And 'Spain's salvation'? Others after you
    Will make that hollow vessel boom as loud.
    Virtue? Keeping faith? All worthless baubles,
    Tarnished already in Carlos the Fifth's time.
    You're no fool – must we fetch a doctor to all
    This sickly sentiment? When you were still
    Sucking on your nurse's teat, we'd long since
    Burst your balloon, with pins or underfoot,
    And with howls of glee quite free of conscience,
    Let all the air out of such arrant nonsense!

RUY BLAS:
    But my lord –

DON SALLUSTO: (*With an icy smile.*)
                Yes, you really are amazing.
    (*Suddenly curt and imperious.*)
    Now, let us turn to matters of import.
    Tomorrow you are to wait for me all morning
    There at the house I gave you. The thing I do
    Now will bring my business to a close.
    The mutes alone should be on hand to serve us.
    See there's a carriage standing at the ready

Hidden in the garden beneath the trees –
I'll arrange relays. Do all this to the letter.
You'll be needing money – I'll have some sent.

RUY BLAS:

My lord, I will do everything you want
But swear to me first that in all this business
The Queen has no part.

DON SALLUSTO: (*He has been toying with an ivory knife on the table and now half turns.*)

Are you trying to meddle?

RUY BLAS: (*Recoiling.*)

You terrify me! What kind of man are you?
To drag me towards an abyss I can't see,
A pawn merely – and to what fearful use?
Something monstrous squats inside your head
Labouring to be born – have pity, sir!
There's something I must tell you – something you weren't
To have known before – I'm in love with the queen!

DON SALLUSTO: (*Coldly.*)

I knew that.

RUY BLAS: You knew?

DON SALLUSTO: Of course I did. What of it?

RUY BLAS:

(*Propping himself up against the wall and as if to himself.*)
He knew. So all this torture has been a game!
And what cruel end does this brute have prepared?
(*Raising his eyes to heaven.*)
Almighty God, can it be Your will I endure
This pain? Spare me, Lord!

DON SALLUSTO: Enough of these dreams!
Really, my man, just who do you think you are?
It's too droll! The end I pursue – that only
I need know – is happier for you than you
Imagine. Keep calm. Do everything I say.
I told you before and tell you once again
I desire your welfare. Everything's in hand.

And anyway, these heartaches, what of them?
Something we all go through – over in a day.
Here the fate of an empire is at stake,
Next to which yours... Look, I'd like to tell you
But do show some shred of intelligence –
Be what you are: I am a good, gentle master,
But a lackey, damn it, of fine clay or coarse,
Is but a vessel I fill with what I please.
You fellows, dear boy, are what we make you:
It may suit the designs of your master's heart
To disguise you one moment, unmask you the next –
At present you're a lord, a pure invention
I have made of you with all the trappings;
But the actor must not forget who he is:
My lackey, whose part now is to woo the queen
Just as if I'd said, 'Hop up on my carriage.'
Come now, be sensible!

RUY BLAS: (*Who has been listening to him in bewilderment and
as if unable to believe his ears.*)
            Merciful God!
What is my crime that you punish me like this?
Heavenly Judge, what have I done? As Father
You would not wish to see a man despair.
See then my plight! – I have done no wrong, my lord,
And yet deliberately, and solely to watch
Your hapless victim writhe in agony,
You have flung me into this pit of darkness,
And, to wreak some private revenge, have put
A loyal wretch who is in love on the rack!
(*To himself.*) For revenge it is, yes, that much is certain,
And on the queen, I'd lay my life on it.
What shall I do? Go tell her everything?
God! And so become for her an object
Of disgust, of horror, the wicked servingman
Who plays a double game and, in the end,
Is bludgeoned for his villainy off the stage?
Never! – My mind turns. I'm starting to rave!
(*A pause. As in a dream:*)

See, dear God, what stands there all prepared:
An instrument of fear built in the darkness
Bristling with a mass of spokes and moving parts;
Now, in order to see if it works, they hurl
Against the wheel a liveried slave, a thing,
And set it in motion. All at once observe
How, from below, blood-stained scraps emerge –
A crushed skull, a heart still warm and steaming –
But note how at this no-one turns a hair
Though they see now, despite this name of lackey,
That inside that livery there had been a man!
(*Turning to DON SALLUSTO.*)
But there's still time, my lord, there truly is –
That dreadful wheel has not begun to turn.
(*Throwing himself at DON SALLUSTO's feet.*)
Spare me, sir! Have pity! Have pity on her!
I've served you faithfully – I always have,
You've often said so. On my knees I beg you,
Mercy, sir!

DON SALLUSTO: This is growing most tiresome!
The man will just never get it into his head –

RUY BLAS: (*Crawling at his feet.*)
Mercy!

DON SALLUSTO: No more of this, my master! Enough!
(*Turning towards the window.*)
There's a cold draught coming from that window.
You can't have closed it properly.
(*He goes and closes it himself.*)

RUY BLAS: (*Getting to his feet.*)   Enough?
Yes, and plenty! I am Duke of Olmedo,
Wield absolute power and refuse to let you
Crush me underfoot!

DON SALLUSTO: I beg your pardon?
Ruy Blas, Duke of Olmedo? Open your eyes!
Without Bazan there first, both names are lies!

RUY BLAS:
I'll have you arrested –

DON SALLUSTO: I'll reveal what you are.

RUY BLAS: (*At a loss.*)
But –

DON SALLUSTO: – then you'll expose me? We'd sink
    together.
I foresaw all this. Your crowing's premature.

RUY BLAS:
I'll deny everything!

DON SALLUSTO: You're so naive!

RUY BLAS:
You've no proof!

DON SALLUSTO: And you've a short memory.
Believe me: my words and actions coincide.
You are but the glove, I the hand inside.
(*Approaching RUY BLAS and lowering his voice.*)
If you don't obey, if tomorrow you are not
At the house with everything I need prepared,
If one word of all this crosses your lips,
Or you show by a look or sign what you know,
Then, for your folly, she for whom you fear
Will be branded whore in every public place;
Second, she'll receive a certain paper
Sealed and which I keep under lock and key,
Written in a hand – perhaps you remember? –
And signed – you must surely know who signed it –
In which she will read these words as I recall:
'I, Ruy Blas, lackey to his lordship
The Marquess of Finlas, vow at all times
And in all places, both public and private,
To serve the said lord in all dutifulness
As a true retainer of his noble house.'

RUY BLAS: (*Broken and hoarse-voiced.*)
Stop! I'll do whatever you want in that case.

(*The upstage doors open and the PRIVY COUNCILLORS
re-enter. DON SALLUSTO quickly wraps himself up in his
cloak.*)

DON SALLUSTO:
  They're coming.
  (*Loud and bowing low to RUY BLAS.*)
                  I am your humble servant, your Grace.

End of Act Three

ACT FOUR

(Don Cesar)

A small, dark room richly decorated. Both panelling and furniture are gilt in the old style. The walls are covered with hangings made of scarlet crushed velvet that glitters in places; this is also on the backs of the armchairs where it is gathered into vertical pleats by means of large golden galloons. Upstage there is a double door. Stage left, in a cant, there is a large fireplace carved according to the fashion of Philip II with an escutcheon of wrought iron inside. In the cant opposite there is a small low door that leads to a dark closet. Left and high up there is the one and only window decorated with small bars and a lower awning as with prison windows. On the wall there are some old smoke-blackened portraits barely discernible in places. In addition: a clothes-chest with a Venetian mirror, large Philip IV armchairs, against the wall a highly ornate cupboard, a square table with writing materials and, in the corner, a small round table with gilt feet.

It is morning. When the curtain rises, an agitated RUY BLAS, dressed in black and without his cloak and Golden Fleece, is pacing the room. Standing motionless upstage and as if awaiting orders, is his PAGE.

RUY BLAS: (*Aside.*)

What's to be done? – First, and above all else,
Her – only her: should they dash my brains out
Against a wall, hang me or hurl me down
To hell, I must save her! Yes – but how?
To surrender up my life – my heart, my soul –
Were easy, a trifle, but to break these coils!
What are they? Where? I must and can only guess
At the web this man has spun. Out of darkness
He appears, only to merge back into the night.
What is he doing there? – Let me not remember
How I pleaded with him for myself at first!
Such a coward! A fool, too, for the man is

Evil, his malice deep-rooted, no doubt of that –
But to think this demon, his prey between his jaws
Bloodied and torn, would have pity on his lackey?
Release the Queen? Can beasts be brought to tears!
But at all costs I must save her for it's I,
Wretched man, who am the cause of her
Undoing. – I am finished. To fall from such a height!
Sink again to such depths! Was it all a dream? –
She must get free of him! But he, the traitor,
What door will he use, what secret entrance
Known only to him? Master of this house,
He lords it, too, over me – life and soul:
He has the keys to each and every lock,
Can come and go at will and, when night falls,
Trample on my heart just as he does this floor –
Did I not dream this? Yes! The mind grows confused
When fate lets loose her arrows at such speed:
Not one helpful thought in my distraught brain!
Dear God, how proud I was of my mind which now,
Swept up in a storm of fear and anger,
Twists and twirls: a thin reed in a gale!
Think hard! What can I do? – First prevent her
From leaving the palace – that, I'm certain,
Must be the snare. – I walk in darkness, chasms
On all sides – I sense but cannot see the abyss!
But that I'll do – keep her at the palace.
I must warn her, of course, without delay –
But whom can I trust? No-one!
(*Sinking momentarily into a despondent reverie, he then
suddenly looks up.*)
                                        Don Guritan!
Yes! He loves her. And he's loyal.
(*Signalling the page to approach.*)   Page, come here!
(*In a low voice.*) Go straightway to don Guritan. Present
My apologies, then tell him he should go
To the Queen immediately and entreat her
In my name, as in his, on no account
To leave the palace for the space of three days.

No matter what is said or comes to pass,
She should not go out. Now run! (*Recalling the page.*)
                                 No, wait! Here –
(*Fetching paper and pen, then writing on his knee.*)
He should give this note to the Queen, and take care:
'Believe don Guritan and do what he says.'
(*Folding the paper and giving it to the PAGE.*)
As regards this duel, say I'm in the wrong,
That I kneel before him, beg compassion
In my distress and urge he go straightway
And implore the Queen – say I'll apologise
To him in public – not to venture forth
Whatever happens – she's in grave danger –
For at least three days. Do this to the letter.
Go! Beware lest your face betray your business.

PAGE:

Good master, for you there's nothing I'd not do.

RUY BLAS:

Run then, good page! You're sure you understand?

PAGE:

Yes, sir. My lord may rest easy in his mind.

(*PAGE exits.*)

RUY BLAS: (*Sitting.*)

I do feel calmer. But, like a madman,
My mind gropes for thoughts that dissolve like mist.
But this safeguard cannot fail – don Guritan –
Do I need to wait now for don Sallusto?
No. I'll not be here. That should stay his hand
A good day. I'll go to some church and there
Implore the help of God: He'll hear my prayer.

(*He fetches his hat from a small table and rings a bell. His two black manservants, the MUTES, appear in the upstage doorway dressed in light green velvet with gold brocade and wearing pleated coats with large tails.*)

I am going out. Soon a man will arrive –
He'll let him*self* in – whose actions may suggest

He were master of the house. Give him free rein.
And if anyone else comes... (*After a moment's hesitation.*)
                well, let them in.

(*He dismisses them with a gesture. They signal their obedience
with a bow and exit. He stands alone a moment, then also
exits. As the door closes behind him, there is a loud noise of
someone sliding down the chimney. Suddenly a man wearing
a tattered cloak tumbles into the fireplace. It is DON CESAR.
He looks fearful, dazed and yet triumphant. He is breathing
heavily. Standing up and rubbing the leg on which he fell, he
comes out into the room, hat in hand and bowing low.*)

DON CESAR:

Please, no ceremony! It's only me.
Just passing through, so to speak. Frightfully
Sorry to interrupt your conversation –
Please, do continue – pretend I'm not here –
My entrance was, I regret, a trifle rude...
(*Stooping in the middle of the room, he notices that he is
alone.*)
No-one here? Perched on the roof a moment
Ago, I thought I heard voices... Not a soul.
(*Stretching himself out in an armchair.*)
Excellent! There's nothing like privacy
For straightening out one's thoughts. What a time
I've had! Drenched in marvels like a drowned rat!
Chapter One: Seized By The Secret Police!
Two: Hustled Aboard Ship – pure farce, that was;
Three: Pirates! Four: A Strange City – still sore
From the bruises given me there; Five: In Which
Our Hero's Virtue Is Put To The Test –
Like yellow satin was that Delilah's skin;
Six: Escape From Prison! Seven: On The Run;
And finally Eight: My Return To Spain.
But then – Part Two – what a novel! – the day
I get back, whom do I meet but those same rogues
Who'd started it all! So: Desperate Flight!
Furious Pursuit! I Leap Over A Wall!
I Espy A House Hidden In The Trees –

I make for house unseen, first climb a shed
And, like a tom-cat, from thence to the roof –
Last chapter: In Which I Enter The Bosom
Of The Family Via The Chimney
And Introduce Myself – tearing meanwhile
My newest cloak that hangs now limp and in rags...
Oh, Sallusto, you're the prince of villains!
(*He looks at himself in the little Venetian mirror on the large chest with the sculpted drawers. Taking off his cloak, he admires his pink satin doublet, now threadbare, torn and patched.*)
My doublet has stuck with me through thick and thin,
Still hangs by a thread –
(*His hand reaches suddenly for his leg and he glances at the chimney.*)
　　　　　　　　　What a fall that was!
Hurts like the devil...what do we have here?
(*He opens the drawers of the chest and finds in one of them a cloak of light green velvet embroidered with gold, the same one DON SALLUSTO gave RUY BLAS. He examines it, comparing it to his own.*)
A marked improvement on mine, I must confess.
(*Having carefully folded his old cloak, put it in the chest and shoved his hat under it, he throws the green one over his shoulders, closes the drawer and proudly struts about.*)
See if I care! I'm back and all is well.
Dearest cousin, you wished to pack me off
To Africa, where tigers turn men into mice
But I'll see you roast on a spit in hell...
Just as soon as I've had something to eat.
With a train of vicious-looking rogues in tow
Able to smell a scaffold a league away,
I'll turn up at your door and, reassuming
My true name, will hand you over to all
My drooling creditors and their ravening brood.
(*He notices in the corner a magnificent pair of boots complete with lace trim. He promptly kicks off his old shoes and, without more ado, puts them on.*)

But first what's this hole he's landed me in now?
(*He explores the room.*)
Perfect setting for a tragedy! Strange:
Doors closed, windows barred – veritable dungeon.
And the entrance to this charming residence
Is down through the neck like a bottle of wine.
(*With a sigh.*)
A good wine, now – ah, that would be something!
(*Seeing the little door on the right, he opens it and quickly goes in, re-emerging with gestures of astonishment.*)
Wonders unceasing: a room leading nowhere
Also bolted and barred!
(*Goes to upstage door, half-opens it, then, closing it, returns downstage.*)
                              No-one about.
Where in hell's name am I? Well, at least
I've shaken off those bloodhounds – so why worry?
Why run scared and let a house get you down
The like you've never come across before?
(*He returns to the armchair and sits, yawns but then stands again almost immediately.*)
Damnation, but this place gets on my nerves!
(*Noticing a little wall cupboard set in the cant, he goes to examine it.*)
What's this? For storing books? So it would seem –
(*Opens it and discovers it to be a well-stocked larder.*)
No! A pie! Some wine! A water-melon –
The very thing! Emergency supplies!
Six flagons – (*Examines them.*) wisely chosen – Worthy
    house!
Please forgive me – I take back all I said.
(*Fetching a small round table from the corner, he brings it downstage and, in joyful mood, loads it with everything out of the cupboard – the bottles, dishes, etc – adding a glass, a plate and cutlery. He then takes up one of the bottles.*)
This 'volume' first. (*Fills glass and drains it one draught.*)
                              Yes! An excellent work,
Its author that famous poet: Summer Sun!

The best wine of Spain is not of ruddier hue –
(*Sits, pours himself a second glass and drinks.*)
Puts reading in the shade – give me something
With more spirit any day! (*Drinks.*) Ah! Lethe-wards
I sink – but first I'll eat.
(*Making a start on the pie.*) Foiled Sallusto's
Minions all right! Stone cold the scent by now.
Mm – a right royal pie! And if by any chance
The owner should, er –
(*Glancing at chimney.*)   drop in –
(*Fetches a glass and place setting from the buffet and places
    them on the table.*)   – he can be my guest!
Just as long as he doesn't kick me out –
I'd best eat up.
(*Doubling the size of his mouthfuls.*)
                        Once I have dined, I'll make
A tour of the house. Who *could* the owner be?
I'll lay any odds that he's a lady's man:
Only a woman could be behind all this.
But what harm am I doing? I don't ask much:
Just your good, old-fashioned hospitality.
To start with, a scoundrel wouldn't stock such wine;
Then, if he comes, I'll do the proper thing
And introduce myself – ah, that'll drive you
Wild, won't it, dearest cousin? 'What did you say?
Not that bohemian, that tramp, that cutthroat,
Zafari? That down-and-out?' – 'Introducing…
Cesar de Bazan! – Don Sallusto's cousin!'
A thunderbolt! Madrid a-buzz with the news:
'When did he get back? This morning? Last night?'
Uproar everywhere! 'Don Cesar! We'd forgotten –
But now see him fall from out a cloudless sky!'
Don Cesar de Bazan – yes, sirs, 'tis I!
'An age since we last thought or spoke of him –
'So he's not dead?' Ladies and gentlemen, he lives!
'Dammit!' say the men. 'Ooh la-la!' the ladies.
You saunter home, the crowds draw back and whisper –
And three hundred creditors howl for your blood!

That's the part for me! – if I had the money.
(*A noise at the door.*)
Someone's coming! To kick me out, I bet,
Like some common cur. Too bad! Show them, Cesar,
The stuff you're made of!
(*He wraps himself up to his eyes in his cloak. The upstage door opens and a liveried servant enters carrying a large satchel on his back.*)
(*Looking the LACKEY up and down.*)

                       Whom is it, friend, you seek?

(*Aside.*) Plenty of swagger – I walk on thin ice.

LACKEY:
Don Cesar de Bazan?

DON CESAR:(*Aside.*)   This fellow's got sharp eyes!
(*Uncovers face, aloud:*)
Don Cesar? The very same!

LACKEY: Cesar de Bazan –
You are he?

DON CESAR: Yes, dammit, yes! I know who I am –
Cesar's my name. The one and only Count
Of…

LACKEY: (*Putting his satchel on the armchair.*)
        Please be good enough to check the amount.

DON CESAR: (*Aside, flabbergasted.*)
Money? Well, I'll be blowed! (*Aloud.*) Now look, old chum –

LACKEY:
Please count it, sir. This bag contains the sum
I was told to bring.

DON CESAR: (*Assuming a serious air.*)
               I see. Good. (*Aside.*) How queer!
I'd give a lot to know… but why interfere
With such a pretty tale – and so timely, too.
(*Aloud.*) Receipt?

LACKEY: No, sir.

DON CESAR: (*Indicating the table.*)
               Put it down – there will do.

(*The LACKEY obeys.*)
From whom... ?

LACKEY: That, *sir* will know.

DON CESAR: Of course! But pray –

LACKEY:
This money comes – yes, that's what I'm to say –
From you know whom and is for you know what.

DON CESAR: (*Nodding sagely.*)
Ah!

LACKEY: We're to guard our tongues or else, the garrotte!
Shh!

DON CESAR: Shh! 'This money comes...' Ah, ravish my ear
And say it again!

LACKEY: This money...

DON CESAR: Crystal clear!
... comes from *I* know whom –

LACKEY: – and *is* for you know what.
We're to –

DON CESAR: Both of us!

LACKEY: (*Pointing to his tongue.*)
                – guard our –

DON CESAR: – tie it in a knot –
I follow perfectly.

LACKEY: That's more than I can say.

DON CESAR:
Come, now!

LACKEY: But you *do*. Me, I just obey.

DON CESAR:
Dammit, man –

LACKEY: No matter. It's enough *you* do.

DON CESAR:
Understand? Of course. And under...take it, too.
Money's simple when it falls into your lap.

LACKEY:
Shh!

DON CESAR: Shh! No loose talk! Tongues must not flap –

LACKEY:
Please! count it, sir.

DON CESAR: Who do you take me for?
(*Admiring the money bag's rotund shape.*)
A fine belly!

LACKEY: But –

DON CESAR: Mistrust's a very whore!

LACKEY:
The gold is in sovereigns which come in both
Double doubloons, weighing in at seven gross
And thirty-six grains, and doubloons eight ounce apiece.
The silver you'll find comes in cross-maries.

(*DON CESAR meanwhile undoes the bag and takes out several pouches of gold and silver which he opens and empties admiringly onto the table; he then begins thrusting his hands into the pouches and filling his pockets with doubloons. He pauses a moment:*)

DON CESAR: (*Aside.*)
See my novel's final fantasy unfold:
In Which Hero Dies For Love Drowned In Gold!
(*He resumes filling his pockets.*)
I'm the crammed galleon of some conquistador!

(*Filling one pocket, he passes to the next and so on until it becomes a quest for more pockets, during which he appears to have quite forgotten the LACKEY who looks on impassively.*)

LACKEY:
I await further orders.

DON CESAR: (*Turning.*) From me? What for?

LACKEY:
I'm to do you know what, but which I don't
Except it's crucial and can't be postponed...

DON CESAR: (*Putting on a knowing air.*)
Of course! It's private – yet it's public, too –

LACKEY:
>...but must be done now, without further ado –
>This much I'm to say.

DON CESAR: (*Slapping him on the back.*)
>   And I thank you for it!
>You have served me faithfully.

LACKEY: Further support,
>So nothing miscarry, my master bids me offer.

DON CESAR:
>A gentleman, clearly, to go to so much bother.
>We must do as he says. (*Aside.*) Hang me if I know
>What orders to give him – !
>(*Loud.*)   Come here! Quid pro quo:
>(*He fills the other glass with wine.*)
>Here, my little galleon – take this on board!

LACKEY:
>But –

DON CESAR: Drink! Down the hatch! – Loyalty's reward.
>(*The LACKEY drinks and DON CESAR refills his glass.*)
>All the way from Oropesa!
>(*Getting the LACKEY to sit and finish his glass, DON CESAR again refills it.*)
>   Come, let's converse!
>(*Aside.*) His eyes shine already – like the gold in my purse.
>(*Aloud and lolling on his chair.*)
>We are naught, my friend, but a plume of black smoke
>Above that raging fire our passions provoke.
>(*Pouring the LACKEY another glass.*)
>I'm talking nonsense of course: smoke that rises
>Up, drawn by the azure blue of the skies, is
>Quite different to the smoke from a chimney stack:
>The one soars upwards, while Man comes belching back.
>(*Rubbing his leg.*)
>Man is leaden – drink up! –
>(*Refilling the two glasses.*)
>   – in matter sunk –
>All your gold's worth less than the song of a drunk.

(*Approaching him with a mysterious air.*)
Take care: the axle cracks if the load's too great –
Walls without foundations soon dilapidate.
Be a good fellow – my collar's come undone –

LACKEY: (*Proudly.*)
I'm no valet, sir.

(*Before DON CESAR can stop him, the LACKEY rings the little bell on the table.*)

DON CESAR: (*Taken aback, aside.*) I wonder who will come –
The master of the house in person perhaps.
My game is up!

(*One of the black MUTES enters. Seized with extreme anxiety, DON CESAR turns to face the opposite end of the room, seeming at a complete loss.*)

LACKEY: (*To the MUTE.*) Kindly fasten the straps
On my lord's cloak.

(*The MUTE goes gravely towards DON CESAR, who looks at him as if dumbstruck, buckles the collar of his cloak, bows and then exits, leaving DON CESAR in a state of frozen terror.*)

DON CESAR: (*Aside.*) I swear I've landed up
In the den of none other than Beelzebub!
(*Coming downstage and pacing up and down.*)
Swim with the tide, Cesar, take what's given you:
A chestful of gold to run your fingers through…
But what will I do with it?
(*Turning back to the LACKEY who is still sitting at the table, drinking and beginning to sway unsteadily on his chair.*)
(*Loud.*)   One moment, please.
(*Aside.*) I could pay my debts – No! – But it *would* appease
My creditors if I greased their dirty palms
By giving them a little – in advance…?
A waste of grease! What, scurvy palms like theirs?
The very thought! Nothing there is that snares
A man's soul more than money, stuffs his mind
With bourgeois attitudes, all grasp and grind,

I don't care if Hannibal who conquered Rome
Was such a man's ancestor... I'd be thrown
To the wolves if ever it got out I'd paid
My debts!

LACKEY: (*Draining his glass.*)
          What are my orders, sir?

DON CESAR: I'm much afraid
You'll have to wait. Help yourself – on the house –
I must meditate.
(*The LACKEY resumes drinking while DON CESAR returns
to his reflections. Suddenly he smacks his forehead as if struck
by an idea.*)
          I know what! (*To LACKEY.*) Come, rouse
Yourself and fill your pockets with these coins.
(*The LACKEY staggers to his feet and starts filling the pockets
of his tunic as instructed, helped by DON CESAR who
continues speaking the while.*)
There's a narrow house in that alley which adjoins
One end of the Plaza Major – know where I mean?
Number nine. Nice place – were it not there's no pane
In the right-hand window, just a paper patch.

LACKEY:
An eye-patch, eh? The haunt of sailors, perhaps?

DON CESAR:
Gentlemen! To whom the house roguishly winks.
Watch out on the stairs: steeper than one thinks –

LACKEY:
A ladder?

DON CESAR: Sort of. You could really come a cropper.
Upstairs there lives this lady, a cap on top of
A haystack of red hair – stands out in a crowd,
I tell you, though she's quite petite; and I'm proud
To say this charming creature is – (another
Reason you're to treat her with respect) – my lover,
The black-eyed Lucinda, who, before the Pope, danced
The fandango one night – to her you should advance
Ten times ten ducats – say they come from me.

Then, nearby, in a hovel you will see
This red-nosed, pot-bellied devil of a fellow,
An ancient hat that's now a faded yellow
Pulled about his ears, from which there droops
One tragic feather – abject when he stoops –
Rapier on hip, rags on back: you should pay
This clown six piastres; then make your way
To the crossroads further on where you'll find
An inn on the corner, a hole black with grime
But as full of song as a forest glade in spring;
There in the doorway, pipe in one hand, drink
In the other, you'll see this man – he's always there –
A gentleman, mind, you'll never hear him swear,
A man of fashion – on that you may depend –
His name, Goulatromba, and my bosom friend.
For him thirty crowns – say, once he's drunk these
I'll give him more – if he asks me on his knees.
Pay these rogues in the cleanest coins you've got
But don't be surprised if they gawp at you.

LACKEY: Then what?

DON CESAR:
The rest is yours. Let's see, the final chapter...

LACKEY:
What are my orders then, my lord?

DON CESAR: To adapt your
Deeds to your fortune: get drunk, you imbecile!
Smash lots of cups, be noisy, shout and squeal,
And don't go home till tomorrow – late at night.

LACKEY:
I hear and –

DON CESAR: Away!
(*LACKEY heads in a zigzag for the door.*)
(*Aside.*)   The man's a Muscovite:
As canned as a cossack! (*Loud.*) Oh, and on your way
You'll pick up a train of the usual waifs and strays:
As a mark of respect for what you have received,
Behave like a gentleman and pay no heed

If you chance to drop the odd crown or two –
Let them fall! And if any of this crew
Of scullions, students or rogues you'll have in tow
Should pick them up, let them! Rather than show
Them your teeth, show them instead understanding,
Even if they filch some by putting their hand in
Your pockets – remember: like us they're only human.
Also, in this vale of tears, to illumine
Others' darkness and spread a little cheer
Is an iron rule of life. (*Sadly.*) Besides, my fear
Is all those fellows may be hanged one day:
They too deserve some respect. So – away!
(*LACKEY exits. Alone, DON CESAR sits down once more,
rests his elbows on the table and appears to be plunged in
thought.*)
It is the duty of every wise man's son
To put his money to good use: this gives me one
Whole week at least of a life of luxury –
And what's left over I'll give to charity.
But what's the betting it's all a huge mistake
And here's me banking on what they're bound to take
Back from me just as soon as they cotton on
That I got quite the wrong end of the stick and…

(*The upstage door opens again and an old, grey-haired
DUENNA enters wearing a black outer-petticoat and shawl
and carrying a fan. She first addresses DON CESAR from
the doorway.*)

DUENNA: Don
Cesar de Bazan?

DON CESAR: (*Starting out of his reveries.*)
                    Now what? (*Aside.*) Heavens! A bawd!
(*Comes downstage as the DUENNA upstage curtsies low.*)
Satan or Sallusto, you can rest assured,
Have a hand in this! Any minute now
We'll see my cousin come in and take *his* bow –
A duenna!
(*Loud.*)   Don Cesar? I am he. State
Your business.

(*Aside.*)   A crone can often herald a maid.

DUENNA: (*Curtsying and making the sign of the cross.*)
In Jesu's name, the Son everlasting,
Greetings, lord, on this day of solemn fasting.

DON CESAR: (*Aside.*)
A pious start to an amorous conclusion.
(*Loud.*) Amen.

DUENNA: God grant you joy and in profusion!
(*Mysteriously.*)
Did you send to someone, who now sends me to you,
To arrange this night a secret – rendezvous?

DON CESAR:
That's – more than likely.

DUENNA: (*Producing a folded letter which she presents to him but
does not allow him to take.*)   Are you then the beau
Who penned this invitation – the hand you'll know –
To her who loves you? Then had it sent discreetly?

DON CESAR:
Must have done.

DUENNA: Good. Her husband's completely
Antiquated, of course, but nevertheless
She must watch her step and so to this address
I was sent to make enquiries. I don't know
The lady – but you will, of course – although
Her maid did tell me something – quite sufficient –
No names, of course –

DON CESAR: Except for mine.

DUENNA: – she isn't
Stupid – to wit: a lady's been invited
To a tryst by her beloved; but – 'Might it
Be a trap?' she thinks – you can't be too
Careful nowadays, of course – and so to you,
In brief, I'm sent for oral confirmation.

DON CESAR: (*Aside.*)
What an old battle-axe! Such complication
Round – good God! – a simple billet doux!

(*Loud.*) I tell you, I'm your man!

DUENNA: (*Putting the folded note on the table which DON
   CESAR eyes curiously.*)   If that is true
   And you are indeed he, then write the word 'Come'
   On the back of this letter – it can't be done
   In your own hand, though – too incriminating.

DON CESAR:
   For whom? I care not.
   (*Aside.*)   'Come.' How – elevating!
   (*He reaches out to take the letter but it has been resealed and
   the DUENNA will not let him touch it.*)

DUENNA:
   Not to be opened! You should know it by its cover.

DON CESAR:
   Damn it – !
   (*Aside.*)   Here's me, the hotly panting lover...
   Time to play the master –
   (*He rings the bell and one of the MUTES enters.*)
                             Know how to write?
   (*The MUTE signals in the affirmative with his head.*)
   A nod. Lost your tongue? Or a case of stage fright?
   (*The MUTE signals affirmation of the former.*)
   (*Aside.*) Marvellous! – mutes now! Well, on with the show!
   (*Indicating to the MUTE the letter which the DUENNA
   holds ready on the table.*)
   (*Loud.*) There, write 'Come'.
   (*The MUTE obeys. DON CESAR signals the DUENNA to
   take up the letter again, then turns to the MUTE.*)
                             Most obliging. (*Loud.*) Now g

   (*Exit MUTE. The DUENNA, pocketing the letter with a
   mysterious air, approaches DON CESAR once more.*)

DUENNA:
   You'll see her tonight. Is she very beautiful?

DON CESAR:
   A gem!

DUENNA: Her waiting woman arranged it all,
Took me aside in the middle of the mass –
Face of an angel she has, the bonny lass,
But a demon in her eye: a knowing minx!

DON CESAR: (*Aside.*)
She'd do just as nicely by the sound of things!

DUENNA:
Since plain ladies fear the company of fair,
We tend to judge the mistress by her underwear –
By her maid, that is – which leads me to suspect
Your lady's a Venus.

DON CESAR: Perfectly correct!

DUENNA: (*Curtsying before withdrawing.*)
I kiss your hand, sir.

DON CESAR: I'll smear yours with grease –
Take these, you old witch! (*Giving her a fistful of doubloons.*)

DUENNA: (*Pocketing the money.*) Ah, how youth likes to tease!

DON CESAR:
Go now!

DUENNA: (*Curtsying.*) If ever you feel the need again,
San-Isidro convent, Dame Oliva the name.
(*She exits but the door opens again and her head reappears.*)
As you enter the church, third pillar on the right –
That's where I sit.
(*DON CESAR turns round impatiently. The door closes then
opens again and the DUENNA's head reappears.*)
         Remember me tonight
In your prayers, my lord – your lady's on her way.

DON CESAR:
Ahh!
(*He chases her off angrily and the door closes.*)
     Nothing can astound me after today –
Have I landed on the moon? – here I am,
Stuffed with gold, with pie, and now like some ram
Awaiting his ewe! All would seem well so far.
But, as they say, all's well that –

(*The upstage door opens again and DON GURITAN appears with two long, unsheathed swords under his arm.*)

DON GURITAN: Don Cesar?
Don Cesar de Bazan?

DON CESAR: (*Turning and seeing DON GURITAN with the swords.*)   At last! You're right on cue!
So far, so good – but now, for some derring-do.
Dinner, ducats, debauchery, now – a duel!
Cesar, that's me! In the throes of self-renewal!
(*Effusively and with a cheerful flourish DON CESAR greets DON GURITAN who, glaring at him, walks stiffly downstage.*)
That's right, do come in! Pull up a chair – you
Must make yourself at home – relax! I dare you!
(*Refusing DON CESAR's offer of a chair, DON GURITAN remains standing.*)
Delighted to meet you! Er – we could chat a bit –
Let's see now – what's been happening here in Madrid?
Charming place! – Me, I'm a bit out of touch
But Matalobos, Lindamire, they're as much
Admired as ever, I expect? – If you ask
Me, it's not the thief but the stealer of hearts
Who's more to be feared. Women! Ah, they're a bad
Lot who'll addle your brains, believe me, my lad!
Come, talk to me! I could do with some advice:
I'm a walking farce, half dead, full of lice –
A corpse, rather, that's escaped its stinking prison,
An oaf, a ludicrous anachronism
Who's lost half his clothes – d'you know a good draper? –
And just got back from an exotic foreign caper.

DON GURITAN:
You've been away, sir? Well, I'll have you know
I've been away, too, but much further!

DON CESAR: (*Brightening.*)   No!
Really? Where was that – if I might be so bold?

DON GURITAN:
Up there, in the north.

DON CESAR: Most unpleasant. And cold.

Me: down there, where the temperature's hotter.

DON GURITAN:
I'm furious, sir!

DON CESAR: You are? Me, too!

DON GURITAN: And what a
Journey! Twelve hundred leagues!

DON CESAR: Two thousand, me.
And women I've seen of every hue – let's see:
Yellow and green, then black – and even blue.
And the places! Sun-drenched! Heavenly! Two
In particular, Algiers and Tunis, they
Were a delight: a Turkish custom, so they say,
Where men are impaled on hooks above the doors!

DON GURITAN:
I, sir, was gulled!

DON CESAR: I was sold to the Moors!

DON GURITAN:
I was well-nigh banished!

DON CESAR: They well-nigh hanged *me*!

DON GURITAN:
I was sent to Neubourg – oh, the subtlety! –
With a box, inside of which a note that ran:
'Detain this old fool for as long as you can.'

DON CESAR: (*Bursting out with laughter.*)
Perfect! Who was this – ?

DON GURITAN: But I tell you, sir,
Cesar de Bazan will pay for it!

DON CESAR: I'm sure –
What? (*Gravely.*) Ah, I see.

DON GURITAN: There are no bounds to his
Audacity! Why, even now – and this
The last straw – he sent his lackey – to *me* –
In his place to offer an apology!
His serving man! Refused to see him, of course.
Had him thrown in irons. Came in person to force

His master's hand: this don Cesar. – Cesar
De Bazan, you impudent traitor! Where are
You, you rogue? I've come to kill you!

DON CESAR: (*With continuing gravity.*)   Here I am.

DON GURITAN:
You, sir? Do you jest?

DON CESAR: (*Bowing.*)   Don Cesar de Bazan!

DON GURITAN:
Again?

DON CESAR: That's right. Once again!

DON GURITAN: I've no doubt
You think you're droll. In truth, you sing, sir, out
Of tune. Kindly cease!

DON CESAR: And you – carry on!
I find you most amusing! A paragon
Of jealousy for whom my heart is bleeding!
For greater by far's the suffering *we* bring
Upon ourselves than what others bring our way –
Rather a poor man than a miser any day,
Or a cuckold than devoured by jealousy!
But you, sir, are both. And why? Well, you see,
Tonight I'm expecting a visit from your wife.

DON GURITAN:
My wife?

DON CESAR: (*Nodding.*)

DON GURITAN: I'm not married.

DON CESAR: (*A sceptical gesture.*)

DON GURITAN: I swear it! On my life!

DON CESAR: Not married? Then why all this perturbation?
The moment you first entered your imitation
Of a raging husband – or snivelling tiger –
So took me in, was so convincing that, like a
Simpleton, I offered you my treasure –
Namely gave you advice – *and* in good measure!
But, if you're *not* her husband, then why on earth

Like some bloated bullfrog d'you cause me such mirth?

DON GURITAN:

Sir, I warn you, you'll drive me to distraction!

DON CESAR:

Pooh!

DON GURITAN: You've gone too far!

DON CESAR: Yes?

DON GURITAN: I want satisfaction!

(*DON CESAR turns his mocking attention to DON GURITAN's shoes which are hidden beneath cascades of ribbon according to the latest fashion.*)

DON CESAR:

There was a time when it was all the rage
To tie ribbons on your head. But now is the age
Of the coiffured foot – very *à la mode!*

DON GURITAN:

We'll fight!

DON CESAR: (*Coolly.*) We will?

DON GURITAN: Cesar or no, you goad
Me so that I'll start with you!

DON CESAR: Best be sure
You can finish with me, too.

DON GURITAN: With you? You're
A dandy! I'll dispatch you straight!

(*DON GURITAN gives him one of the swords.*)

DON CESAR: (*Twirling the sword.*)   Have a care:
Duelling's my forte – best say a prayer.

DON GURITAN:

The place?

DON CESAR: Outside behind the wall the street's
As quiet as – the grave?

DON GURITAN:(*Testing the point of his sword on the floor.*)
                     Your death but precedes
Cesar's.

DON CESAR: You're sure of that?

DON GURITAN: That's what I said.

DON CESAR: (*Bending his sword now in turn.*)
Kill don Cesar once one of *us* is dead,
And you're not the fool I take you for.

DON GURITAN: Let's go!

(*They exit. The sound of their departing footsteps. A small, concealed door in the right-hand wall opens and DON SALLUSTO enters. He is dressed in a green verging on black. He seems anxious and preoccupied, looking about him and listening uneasily.*)

DON SALLUSTO:
Nothing ready! (*Seeing the table with the food on it.*)
What's the meaning of this?
(*Listens at the door by which DON CESAR and DON GURITAN left.*)
Who's making that din? (*Begins to pace up and down.*)
Gudiel spied the page
Leaving the house today, trailed him as far
As don Guritan's where – no sign of Ruy Blas! –
Hellfire! He's hatched some plot to counter
Mine – a warning, perhaps, don Guritan
Should take to the Queen – the wretched mutes
Can tell me nothing – but that must be it, yes –
I hadn't reckoned with this don Guritan –

(*DON CESAR re-enters, throws the drawn sword onto an armchair, then sees DON SALLUSTO.*)

DON CESAR:
So! I thought as much – talk of the devil –

DON SALLUSTO: (*Spinning round, horrified.*)
Don Cesar!

DON CESAR: (*Bursting out laughing.*)
What fearsome web have you spun
That I've now blundered into and torn to shreds?

DON SALLUSTO: (*Aside.*)
Everything ruined!

DON CESAR: (*Laughing.*) All day I've been buzzing
Back and forth through your cobwebbed handiwork
So that all your well-strung nets, now in tatters,
Are hanging limply down. And such delight
It has given me, too!

DON SALLUSTO: (*Aside.*) What can the dolt have done?

DON CESAR: (*Laughing more and more loudly.*)
Your man with the money bag – he was the first –
With his 'you-know-what' and his 'you-know-whom' –
Priceless!

DON SALLUSTO: And?

DON CESAR: I got him drunk.

DON SALLUSTO: And the cash?

DON CESAR: (*Majestically.*)
Sent to various persons in the form of gifts.
Dammit, a man has friends, you know!

DON SALLUSTO: You're wrong
To think –

DON CESAR: (*Shaking his breeches.*)
        Filled my own pockets first, of course.
(*Starts laughing again.*)
And then the lady –

DON SALLUSTO: (*With a start.*) Yes?

DON CESAR: (*Seeing his anxiety.*) – whom you clearly know –
(*DON SALLUSTO listens with redoubled anxiety. DON
CESAR, laughing, continues:*)
Sends me this duenna – a frightful old hag
Whose bushy beard and protruding bulbous nose –

DON SALLUSTO:
Why?

DON CESAR: To make quite sure – oh, so discreetly! –
It was indeed Cesar who'd asked her to – 'come'.

DON SALLUSTO:
(*Aside.*) Damn her!
(*Loud.*)   So! And – what answer did you give?

DON CESAR:
  I said yes, of course, and that I couldn't wait!

DON SALLUSTO: (*Aside.*)
  It may be not everything is lost after all.

DON CESAR:
  Last came Jack the Giant-killer – by his lights at least –
  But who challenged me in the name of don Guritan –
  (*DON SALLUSTO gives a start.*)
  One who, in his wisdom, had earlier refused
  To see Cesar's page or the message he bore
  But instead came here to seek satisfaction
  Of me for –

DON SALLUSTO: So what did you do?

DON CESAR: I killed the goose.

DON SALLUSTO:
  Really?

DON CESAR: Really. He's dying right now – out there
  Beneath the wall.

DON SALLUSTO: You're sure?

DON CESAR: I'm afraid so.

DON SALLUSTO: (*Aside.*)
  Thank God for that! He hasn't marred a thing –
  Quite the opposite. But now I must be shot
  Of this, my blundering lieutenant. As for
  The money, that's a trifle.
  (*Loud.*)   Quite amazing!
  And you've seen no-one else?

DON CESAR: No – but I will!
  I intend more: to blazon my name throughout
  Madrid till a scandal bursts that would blacken snow!
  Of this you may be sure.

DON SALLUSTO:(*Aside.*) The devil take him!
  (*Quickly going to DON CESAR.*)
  The money you may keep – but leave this house.

DON CESAR:
>Oh, yes! You'd have me followed – I know you!
>And So Once More 'Tis Our Hero's Happy Fate
>This Wat'ry Globe To Circumnavigate!
>No.

DON SALLUSTO: Believe me –

DON CESAR: No! Besides, this dungeon
>Of a place must have a victim, someone trapped
>In your coils – court intrigues all consist,
>Like executions, of predator and prey:
>Up one ladder climbs the condemned, his arms
>Tied, face pinched and pale, while up the other
>Climbs the man in the mask – you, in this case –
>But I'll shake yours till I bring you clattering down!

DON SALLUSTO:
>I swear –

DON CESAR: I'll keep my part in this adventure
>And so foul up everything! You, dear cousin,
>Are quite capable and clever enough
>To manage several puppets on the same string:
>Well, I'm one of them and am here to stay!

DON SALLUSTO:
>Listen –

DON CESAR: Words, words! And as worthless as air!
>What did you *do*? Had me sold to pirates!
>And then? Put some bogus Cesar in my place,
>Thus bringing my name into disrepute!

DON SALLUSTO:
>It was quite by chance –

DON CESAR: Chance!? Chance is a mouthful
>Rogues serve for fools to swallow. Chance be choked!
>Tough if your plans come unstuck, I intend
>To save those here whom you want to destroy.
>I'll shout my name from the rooftops – just you see!
>(*DON CESAR climbs up onto the window frame and peers out.*)

Perfect! Some guards are passing down below –
(*Putting his arm through the bars, he waves it and shouts.*)
Hallo! Up here!

DON SALLUSTO: (*Aside and coming downstage, greatly
    agitated.*)   If he is recognised,
Then all is lost!

(*The guards enter, headed by an officer. DON SALLUSTO
doesn't seem to know which way to turn. Triumphantly DON
CESAR goes up to the OFFICER.*)

DON CESAR: Put down in your report...

DON SALLUSTO: (*Indicating DON CESAR to the officer.*)
That you've caught the famous thief – Matalobos!

DON CESAR: (*Flabbergasted.*)
What!

DON SALLUSTO: (*Aside.*)
      Time, I need time: one day and all is mine.
(*Loud to officer.*)
This is that thief who in broad daylight dares
To enter our homes – lay hold on the villain!

(*The guards seize DON CESAR by his collar.*)

DON CESAR: (*Furious, to DON SALLUSTO.*)
Your servant, sir, but you lie through your teeth!

OFFICER:
Who was it, then, who called us?

DON SALLUSTO: I did.

DON CESAR: The nerve!

OFFICER:
Silence! I think he's right.

DON CESAR: Then you think wrong:
I am don Cesar de Bazan!

DON SALLUSTO: Don Cesar?
Kindly look at his cloak. Under the collar
You'll find the name SALLUSTO clearly stitched –
It is my cloak, one that he's just stolen.
(*The guards pull off the cloak and the OFFICER examines it.*)

OFFICER:
He's right.

DON SALLUSTO: And then the doublet he is wearing –

DON CESAR: (*Aside.*)
Damn you, Sallusto!

DON SALLUSTO: – belongs to the Count
Of Alba from whom he stole it –
(*Pointing out the coat-of-arms on the cuff of the left sleeve.*)
                              – and whose coat-of-arms
You see.

DON CESAR: (*Aside.*) Satan inspires him!

OFFICER: (*Examining the coat-of-arms.*)   Yes, in gold
The two castles –

DON SALLUSTO: – and with the two cauldrons
Of Enriquez and Guzman.
(*In the struggle, some doubloons fall out of DON CESAR's
pockets. DON SALLUSTO points out those remaining and
how they are stuffed in.*)
                              Is this how you'd expect
Honest folk to carry their money?

OFFICER: (*Shaking his head.*)   Humph!

DON CESAR:(*Aside.*)
I'm done for!
(*The guards frisk him and take his money.*)

GUARD: Here are some papers.

DON CESAR: (*Aside.*)   No, not those!
To survive so much and – oh, my billets doux!

OFFICER: (*Examining them.*)
Letters – what's this? – in different hands

DON SALLUSTO: (*Pointing out the addresses.*) But all
Addressed to the Count of Alba!

OFFICER: Yes.

DON CESAR: But –

GUARDS: (*Binding his hands.*)
Caught him! What luck!

(*Another GUARD enters and addresses the OFFICER.*)

GUARD: Outside a man lies murdered –

OFFICER:
And the murderer?

DON SALLUSTO: (*Indicating DON CESAR.*)
                           There he stands!

DON CESAR: (*Aside.*)   That duel!
Oh, here's a tangle!

DON SALLUSTO: When he came in, he had
A sword – look, there it is!

OFFICER: (*Picking up and examining the sword.*)
                           Blood. Very good –
(*To DON CESAR.*)
You're under arrest!
(*Signals the guards to take him away.*)

DON SALLUSTO: (*To DON CESAR as the guards take him out.*)
                           Matalobos? (*The guards stop and turn.*)
                                        Farewell!

DON CESAR: (*Taking a step towards him and fixing him with a stare.*)
A prize villain – you'll be the toast of hell!

End of Act Four

ACT FIVE

(The Tiger and the Lion)

The same room. It is now night. There is a lamp on the table. When the curtain rises, RUY BLAS is alone. He is wearing a long black robe which covers what he has on underneath

RUY BLAS:

The dream I had! Snuffed out! I watched its light
Die slowly as I roamed the streets till dusk –
Peaceful, though, the dark: friendlier to thought
Than the rowdy day. I'm calm now; all is well.
Nothing fearful hangs on these black walls;
The room is in order, cupboards locked and barred;
Upstairs the mutes are sleeping and the house itself
Sleeps soundly too: no need to be afraid.
My page would never fail me, while don Guritan
Can be wholly trusted in all that touches her.
Dear God, I thank Thee already from my heart
For seeing to it she received my warning,
For helping me, Thou who art so just and good,
To protect this angel, outwit don Sallusto,
That nothing come to terrify or hurt her,
And that thus she may be saved – and I may die.
(*He takes out a small phial which he places on the table.*)
Die, wretch – yes, now! The jaws of hell gape wide:
Throw yourself down and purge your soul in fire!
Die in this house, miserably, alone –
(*He opens his robe, beneath which he is wearing the same livery he wore in Act One.*)
Die at the last a slave beneath your shroud.
But if that fiend comes to gloat over his kill,
At least I'll stop him using this dreadful door!
(*Pushes a chair against the secret entrance.*)
My page saw Guritan – of course he did:
When he left the house it was still quite early.
(*Staring at the phial.*)

The sentence passed, the penalty is death
Which I myself will mete out – these few drops
Will hurl on me a massive lid of stone.
No way but this, though – in that, some comfort.
And yet she loved me! Dear God, lend me strength –
I lack the courage – (*He weeps.*) If we had but been left
In peace, sweet Lord!
(*He hides his head in his hands and sobs, then, raising his
head and looking distractedly at the phial.*)
                      The man who sold me this
Asked me what day it was – I couldn't say.
My head, it hurts. This world is evil, cold:
You die and men yawn. And yet she loved me.
What's past is lost forever, will never return –
Her hand in mine, her lips that kissed me here –
(*Touching his forehead.*)
Never will I see my beloved's face again,
My angel, my poor angel, for I must die.
Grace lay hid in every fold of her dress;
To hear her footsteps would shake me to the core;
Her eyes from which my own would drink and reel,
Her smile, her voice, will I really never see,
Never hear them again?   Harsh finality!

(*In torment he reaches for the phial; just as he seizes it, the
upstage door opens and the QUEEN appears. She is dressed
in white but with a dark overmantle, the hood of which is
thrown back so that her pale face is visible. Placing on the
floor the dim lantern which she holds, she moves swiftly towards
RUY BLAS.*)

QUEEN:
Don Cesar!

RUY BLAS: (*Whirling round and quickly wrapping himself in the
    robe which hides his livery.*)
                My God, the Queen! The trap springs shut!
She's caught! (*Loud.*) Oh, Lady!

QUEEN: What dreadful cry is this?
Cesar –

RUY BLAS: Why are you here? Who told you to come?

QUEEN:
Why, you did.

RUY BLAS: I did?

QUEEN: Yes. You sent me –

RUY BLAS: (*Breathlessly.*)   What?
Say quickly!

QUEEN: – a letter.

RUY BLAS: Letter?

QUEEN: Yes.

RUY BLAS: I?

QUEEN:
Written by you – I recognised your hand.

RUY BLAS:
You'll drive me mad – I never wrote a letter!

QUEEN:
Then read this.

(*She takes a note from her bosom and gives it to RUY BLAS who snatches it and then leans over the lamp to read it.*)

RUY BLAS: (*Reading.*) 'I stand in great peril.
Only my Queen can shield me from the deadly
Lightning bolt...' (*Looking aghast and unable to continue.*)

QUEEN: (*Her finger on the line.*) '... come to my house tonight,
Else I am lost.'

RUY BLAS: (*In a weak voice.*) The cunning! Yes, that note!

QUEEN:
'To avoid being recognised, enter the house
By the last door that you will come to. Someone
Of the highest trust will be there to let you in.'

RUY BLAS: (*Aside.*)
I'd quite forgotten it.
(*To the QUEEN in a terrible voice.*) Get out of here!

QUEEN:
I'm going, sir. – But how can you be so cruel?

What is it I have done?

RUY BLAS: What you have done?
Heavens! Put your head in the noose!

QUEEN: How?

RUY BLAS: I can't
Explain. Go now! Quickly!

QUEEN: To be quite sure,
I even went so far as to send a duenna –

RUY BLAS:
God! Each moment that passes, your life gushes
Out – as from an open wound! Please – go!

QUEEN: (*As if struck by a sudden idea.*)
My love is as a mirror – in it I see you:
Some dark hour draws near and you would have me
Out of danger's way – no, I am staying!

RUY BLAS:
My God, the idea! Stay? Now? And of all
Places, here?

QUEEN: You did write this letter, so –

RUY BLAS: (*Lifting his hands up to heaven in despair.*)
Merciful God!

QUEEN: Now you want me to go.

RUY BLAS: (*Taking her hands.*)
Please understand!

QUEEN: Oh, but I think I do:
You wrote in the heat of the moment but now –

RUY BLAS: No! I didn't! Think I'm some demon and fly
This hell! It's you who have been snared, entrapped –
It's true! And closing in, a horde of fiends!
What else can I say? I can't think! You must believe –
Listen – I love you! This you surely know:
To save you from your worst fears coming true
I'd gladly rip the heart from out of my chest!
Do you understand? I love you. Now, go!

QUEEN:
  Don Cesar –

RUY BLAS: Go! – But someone, now I think
  Of it, must have let you in.

QUEEN: Of course.

RUY BLAS:
  In the devil's name, who?

QUEEN: He wore a mask
  And hid against the wall.

RUY BLAS: A mask? But what
  Did he say, this man? Was he tall? What kind
  Of man was he? Oh, speak for heaven's sake!

  (*A masked man dressed in black appears in the upstage door.*)

MASKED MAN:
  It was I.

  (*He removes his mask and the QUEEN and RUY BLAS
  recognise DON SALLUSTO.*)

RUY BLAS: Oh, lady! Fly!

DON SALLUSTO: Fly? Too late!
  Madam de Neubourg is Queen of Spain no more.

QUEEN: (*In horror.*)
  Don Sallusto!

DON SALLUSTO: (*Indicating RUY BLAS.*)
                  Henceforth and for ever
  Your consort is this man.

QUEEN: So it *was* a trap.
  God! – And Cesar…

RUY BLAS: (*In despair.*) Lady! what have you done?

  (*DON SALLUSTO slowly approaches the QUEEN.*)

DON SALLUSTO:
  You are in my power. But first, Your Majesty,
  I'll speak. And gently, too, not in anger.
  I find you here – softly now, and listen –
  Alone with don Cesar, here in his room
  And in the dead of night. This, for a queen,

Would, were it made public, be quite enough
For Rome to declare your marriage null and void –
His Holiness the Pope would be told forthwith.
But if we agree, none of this need happen.
It could all remain secret.
(*Taking a parchment from his pocket, he unrolls it and presents it to the QUEEN.*)
                                        Sign this letter
To His Majesty the King. I will have it sent
By the Grand Equerry to the Notary
In Chief. Next, there is a carriage – in which
I have placed a hoard of gold – right outside.
You're to leave, both of you, now. I will help.
By Toledo and Alcantara you can reach
Portugal, have no fear. Once you are there
You may go where you will – it matters not
To us – we'll turn a blind eye. Do what I say.
So far only I know of this, I swear,
But tomorrow all Madrid if you refuse.
Let's not excite ourselves. You're in my hold.
(*Indicating the table on which there is a writing desk.*)
Your signature, Ma'am. There stand pen and ink.

QUEEN: (*Falling, as if crushed, into a chair.*)
He has me by the throat!

DON SALLUSTO: All I require
Is this, your consent, to bear before the King.
(*Low to RUY BLAS who has been listening but stock-still as if struck by lightning.*)
See how I labour, friend, in your behalf.
(*To the QUEEN.*)
Sign!

QUEEN: (*Trembling and aside.*)
        What should I do?
(*DON SALLUSTO leans over the QUEEN and speaks in her ear while offering her a pen.*)

DON SALLUSTO: Come, what's in a crown?
Happiness? Yours in abundance once it's gone.

I've ordered my men to stay outside. No-one
Knows of this save we three.
(*He tries to put the pen in her hand; she neither takes it nor
pushes it away but, wavering and bewildered, looks at him
fearfully.*)

                  What do you say?
Sign or you strike a blow against yourself:
A public branding, then the cloister –

QUEEN: (*Overwhelmed.*)   Oh, God!

DON SALLUSTO: (*Indicating RUY BLAS.*)
Cesar loves you. He is worthy of you, too:
There's not a nobler house in Spain than his,
I swear – why, he's almost a prince! The lord
Of a mountain fortress, large estates, he is
The duke of Olmedo, Bazan, grandee of Spain –

(*He moves the QUEEN's hand onto the document – trembling
and at a loss, she appears to be about to sign.*)

RUY BLAS: (*As if suddenly waking up.*)
I am a lackey. Ruy Blas is my name.
(*He snatches the pen from the QUEEN's hand and the
document which he tears to pieces.*)
Don't sign, my lady! At last – I can breathe!

QUEEN:
What? Don Cesar?

(*RUY BLAS lets his robe fall to the ground, thus revealing
himself in livery and without a sword.*)

RUY BLAS: My name, I say, is Ruy
Blas and this man is my master. To him –
(*Turning to DON SALLUSTO.*)
I say, treachery ends here! No more deceit!
As for my happiness, I'll have none of it –
A waste of breath, that whispering in my ear –
It's time I woke at last. And furthermore
I say – though throttled in your coils, a snare
I'll never now escape – we make a pair
To shame a beggar! Two, and yet one whole:
I have the garb of lackey – you have the soul!

DON SALLUSTO: (*To the QUEEN coldly.*)
   He's my man, it's true.
   (*To RUY BLAS with authority.*) Not another word!

QUEEN: (*Finally giving vent to a cry of despair and wringing her
      hands.*)
   Merciful Heavens!

DON SALLUSTO: He spoke too soon, that's all.
   (*To the QUEEN in a loud voice, drawing himself up to his
   full height and folding his arms.*)
   Well, well, no matter – now we'll lay all bare.
   I have my revenge more or less. Don't you think?
   Oh, how Madrid will ring with laughter, eh?
   You, who broke my power, I have dethroned;
   To you, who banished me, I do the same –
   I to whom you offered your drudge for wife
   Have given you my lackey to warm your sheets!
   (*A burst of laughter.*)
   The King will soon be dead – then, he can be
   Your husband, too – his love, your meat and drink –
   Your duke, with you his duchess – such foresight there!
   (*Suddenly vicious.*)
   You snapped me like some twig, crushed me underfoot,
   And thought then to sleep soundly? Little fool!

   (*RUY BLAS meanwhile has gone and bolted the upstage
   door. Now, unobserved, he slowly approaches DON
   SALLUSTO from behind. On the word 'fool', when DON
   SALLUSTO is glaring triumphantly at the paralysed
   QUEEN, RUY BLAS seizes DON SALLUSTO's sword by
   the hilt and swiftly unsheathes it.*)

RUY BLAS: (*In high rage and holding SALLUSTO's sword.*)
   You dare insult your Queen? Treason, I cry!
   (*DON SALLUSTO rushes towards the door but RUY BLAS
   bars his way.*)
   Too late: besides it's bolted. Save your strength.
   Until today you've sheltered safe beneath
   The shielding hand of Satan – if, to snatch you
   From my grasp, he'll now appear, let him come!

A snake in the grass? I'll deal with it, no fear.
We're alone. Your men will stay outside. I see
No devil but you, squirming beneath my heel.
Did this man speak to you rudely, my lady?
I'll tell you why: he has no soul – not even
A lackey's. Yesterday, while this brute crushed
The life out of me, how he laughed! He made me
Close a window just to gloat at my pain.
I begged him, I wept – how can I describe – ?
(*To DON SALLUSTO.*)
Angry and aggrieved, now your hour has come?
Plead your case to the moon. I am deaf. Besides,
I can't conceive… Wretch, how dare you! Your Queen –
The sweetest woman – to abuse her to my face?
A man, too, of your intelligence –
You amaze me – that you could think I'd stand
Dumbly by! Now hear me speak! When a traitor,
A conniving villain, no matter what his rank,
Commits certain gross and execrable acts,
Then any man meeting him, whether lord or slave,
May freely spit in such a villain's face,
Reach for a sword, a knife or rope and… God!
Then lackey can turn hangman – yes, why not?

QUEEN:
You mean to kill him?

RUY BLAS: That I must carry out
This task in your presence I deeply deplore
But there's no other way but here and now.
(*He pushes DON SALLUSTO towards the closet.*)
In there, my lord! And pray – if you know how.

DON SALLUSTO:
This is murder!

RUY BLAS: I'd call it something else.

DON SALLUSTO: (*Angrily looking about him.*)
Not one weapon here! (*To RUY BLAS.*)
                 Give me a sword, at least!

RUY BLAS: Marquess, you mock me! I, a gentleman?
Your glove? The vessel you fill with what you please?
I duel? A menial? In slavery's frills?
A rogue who's kicked, who's flogged – a rogue who kills?
For kill you I will, yes, that's certain, sir,
Kill you as one might some cringing, rabid cur!

QUEEN: Spare his life!
(*RUY BLAS seizes DON SALLUSTO, then turns to the QUEEN.*)

RUY BLAS: Before vengeance all must bow.
Not even angels can save this devil now.

QUEEN: (*On her knees.*)
Spare him!

DON SALLUSTO: (*Calling for help.*)
                    I'm being murdered – !

RUY BLAS: No more words!

DON SALLUSTO: (*Throwing himself on RUY BLAS.*)
– Butchered!

RUY BLAS: (*Pushing him into the closet.*)
                    No! You're getting your just deserts!

(*They disappear into the closet and the door closes. The QUEEN, alone, collapses into the chair, barely conscious. After a moment of silence, RUY BLAS re-emerges, pale and without the sword. He takes a few unsteady steps towards the QUEEN who is motionless and stiff, as if made of ice. He then falls onto his knees, his head bent to the ground as if not daring to raise his eyes to her.*)

(*In a low, grave voice.*)
My lady, I must tell you – have no fear,
I'll keep my distance but you must hear the truth.
My treachery, I'm sure, must seem to you
Unspeakable. I'm not as guilty, though,
As you will think. Oh, how can I explain!
I'm not an evil man. At heart I'm honest.
Love was my undoing. But I've no excuse:
I know too well I should have found some way –

I failed, however. It's done, the price paid.
But listen, through it all I truly loved you.

QUEEN:
Sir –

RUY BLAS: Don't be afraid, I'll come no nearer.
I simply want to tell you everything
Exactly as it happened. Oh, believe me,
Your Majesty, I'm not an evil man!
All today I paced the city's streets
Like one deranged – many turned to stare.
Near that hospital you helped to found
I dimly recollect a woman – I'd grown
Delirious by then – silently wiping
The drops of sweat from off my fevered brow –
Oh God, have pity on me! My heart is breaking.

QUEEN:
What do you want?

RUY BLAS: (*Joining his hands as in prayer.*)
                    Oh lady, to be forgiven!

QUEEN:
Never!

RUY BLAS: Never. Are you sure?

QUEEN: Quite. Never!

   (*RUY BLAS stands and walks slowly towards the table where
   he takes up the phial, raises it to his lips and drains it.*)

RUY BLAS:
The flame shed little light. Let it go out.

QUEEN: (*Standing and going quickly to him.*)
What's that?

RUY BLAS: (*Putting the phial down.*)
                    Nothing. Nothing matters now.
No more pain. To you I am a monster.
For me you are a joy. As simple as that.

QUEEN: (*Distraught.*)
Cesar!

RUY BLAS:

Poor angel – to think you loved me once!

QUEEN:

What was in that phial? What have you done?
Tell me! Answer me! I want to know. Speak!
Cesar, I forgive you, love you, believe –

RUY BLAS:

My name is Ruy Blas.

QUEEN: (*Taking him in her arms.*) I forgive you then,
Ruy Blas! But what was it that you took?
Tell me at once! Poison? Heaven forfend!

RUY BLAS: (*Returning her embrace and raising his eyes to
heaven.*)

It was. But Heaven is here – and now! Oh look
Down, great Father, and give a lackey leave
To bless this queen: her love, while he had breath,
Soothed his soul as it writhed upon the tree,
Her pity made it sing at the hour of his death.

QUEEN:

Poison, oh God, which *I* made him drink!
I love you! If I'd forgiven you before – ?

RUY BLAS: (*Failing.*)

I'd have done the same.
(*His voice fades and only the QUEEN's support keeps him
up from falling.*)
                            No. You mustn't think
You were the cause – Farewell! (*Indicating.*)
                            Leave by that door –
Quickly! No-one will know you ever came –
(*He falls and the QUEEN throws herself on his body.*)

QUEEN:

Ruy Blas!

RUY BLAS: (*Reviving momentarily.*)
            The joy – to hear you say my name!

The End